In a Flash

Previous page: Texas Beef Ribs, p. 52
Carne Asada (Mexican Steak), p. 49

In a
Flash

FAST AND FABULOUS BARBECUE MEALS
from the Fire Chef

David Veljacic

Douglas & McIntyre

Vancouver/Toronto/New York

Douglas & McIntyre Ltd.
#201 2323 Quebec Street
Vancouver, British Columbia
V5T 4S7

Canadian Cataloguing in Publication Data

Veljacic, David, 1941–
In a flash

Includes index.
ISBN 1-55054-862-x
1. Barbecue Cookery I. Title.
TX840.B3V452 2001   641.7′6   C2001-910156-2

Editing by Audrey Grescoe
Text design by Cardigan Industries
Typography by Warren Clark
Cover design by Val Speidel
Photography by John Sherlock
Printed and bound in Canada by Friesens

Printed on acid-free paper

The publisher gratefully acknowledges the assistance of the Canada Council and of the British Columbia Ministry of Tourism, Small Business and Culture. The publisher also acknowledges the financial support of the Government of Canada through the Book Publishing Industry Development Program (BPIDP) for its publishing activities.

FOR ALL FIREFIGHTERS EVERYWHERE,

WHO PUT THEIR LIVES ON THE LINE

EVERY DAY FOR THE PUBLIC THEY SERVE

Introduction

Everyone thought barbecue cooking was at its peak in the late nineties when my first book—*The Fire Chef*—appeared. We were all surprised that its popularity grew again in the year 2000. It seems as if every month there are new styles of barbecues and all sorts of equipment and products designed to improve barbecuing and make it easier.

In *The Fire Chef*, I dealt with two methods of cooking over hot coals or a gas fire in the outdoors. In the indirect method, cooking is done on the unfired side of the barbecue. Large cuts of meat or foods with high fat content (ribs, sausages and duck) are cooked this way. As far as some people are concerned, that's what barbecue is—long, slow cooking over indirect heat.

The other method is grilling—quick cooking over direct heat. The direct method is used for smaller cuts of meat or fish and even vegetables and fruits. This is what most of us do on the barbecue. We grill hamburgers, steaks and fish.

Most of the recipes in this book are designed for this direct grilling method. Only a special few require a longer period of indirect cooking. Most of the grilled recipes will allow you to have dinner on the table in a flash—in less than an hour, with a portion of that time often set aside for marinating your meat or fish.

The Balanced BARBECUE Meal

The side dishes in this book are either variations of the traditional mates with grilled foods or have been designed to balance the spiciness or blandness of the entrées. I like spicy foods, but I've learned that many people aren't as adventuresome as I am in that way. Watching guests gulp down water has taught me to serve palate-coolers with dishes loaded with jalapeños or dried red chilies.

Because sugar cools the fire of chilies (much better than water), I serve salsas and salads that are sweet in taste. Often they get their sweetness from fruits. Examples of good coolers are my Papaya and Jicama Salad (page 133) or Arizona Avocado Salad (page 126).

Going the opposite way, if you have a mild or bland entrée, look for a sauce or salsa with some oomph to it, such as Avocado and Bell Pepper Salsa (page 142) or Spicy Dipping Sauce (page 25), which has a tablespoon of crushed red chilies to make you weep.

This book is different from *The Fire Chef* in that some starters, salads and vegetables that complement barbecue dishes are cooked indoors. Many of these can be prepared ahead of time so that you can be in the backyard with your guests as you grill the entrée.

Purchasing
Food Products

Since the book is about cooking in a hurry, I use several prepared products that save me time and have a great deal of flavour to contribute to the dish. These are listed and described in the section In My Pantry. I put out the extra money for top-of-the-line products, which I think have the most flavour and will most enhance what I'm cooking.

Top-of-the-line goes for the main ingredients, too. I can't say it often enough: whether it is meat, poultry, seafood, vegetables or fruit, always purchase high-grade products. In fact, your grocer, butcher and fish merchant are important contributors to the success of your cooking and should be carefully cultivated, as I have mine over many years.

Preparing food that tastes absolutely wonderful does take time (even though we're keeping that to a minimum) along with tender, loving care. Most of the memorable barbecue meals I've eaten were cooked in a backyard by someone who had a deep love for the food he or she was serving and for the family who would eat it.

This book is the result of that kind of love–the love my wife, Patricia, and I shared for barbecue. Pat and I worked on this book together up to the day of her passing. Her contribution to it is immeasurable.

Elementary
BARBECUE

- Oil the grid with a nonstick cooking spray or paper towel dipped in oil before you heat the barbecue.

- Have the lid of a gas barbecue completely open when you are igniting it.

- Always preheat the barbecue. Some manufacturers recommend preheating to 500 to 550°F with all burners set on high, which will take about 10 minutes.

- Grill with the lid closed. Open only to baste or turn food.

- I keep a mixture of water and baking soda in a spray bottle in case of a flare-up. However, some manufacturers of gas barbecues advise against using water, saying you should turn the burners off and move the food to another area of the grid until the flare-up dies down.

- Protect your hands and arms with long-sleeved, heat-proof grill mitts and use long-handled brushes and tools.

- Shut off the barbecue while the food is still on the grid. Close the lid and shut the tank valve before you turn the burners off, so that there will be no gas in the hose, which might leak into the barbecue the next time you light it.

- Keep your barbecue clean. After every use, scrape the grid with a wire-bristle brush and, before barbecuing again, turn the flame on high and scrape the grid again.

- Keep a fire extinguisher handy.

starters

Bell peppers

grilled and filled with YOGURT

A brief time on the grill and you have this light and cheerful starter. Yellow bell peppers are nutritious, containing beta carotene and lots of Vitamin C.

2   medium yellow bell peppers
1 cup   plain yogurt
1   small lime
    salt
    paprika

Leaving the stem on, slice the peppers in half lengthwise. Clean out the seeds and remove as much of the white membrane as possible and set aside.

Put the yogurt in a non-reactive bowl, add the juice of the lime and set aside to reach room temperature.

With the barbecue at medium to high heat (350 to 400°F), grill the peppers directly over the heat, turning them until they just begin to get supple and char slightly.

Remove the peppers to individual small appetizer bowls. Salt the inside of each, fill with yogurt and sprinkle with paprika.

Serves 4

TANDOORI
CHICKEN strips

¾ lb	chicken fillets (10 to 12)
5 tbsp	Tandoori Rub (see page 36)
	olive oil
4	medium limes, cut into wedges
	baguette bread

Pound the fillets out between wax paper to about half their thickness. Sprinkle with the rub and then rub the spices well into the meat. Allow to stand at room temperature for 10 minutes before cooking.

Grill the chicken pieces directly over medium to high heat (350 to 400°F) for about 2 minutes a side. Turn and baste with the olive oil several times.

Serve with lime wedges and sliced baguette bread.

Serves 4

The Indian tandoor is a cylindrical clay oven in which a form of barbecue cooking is done. Skewered meat or poultry is cooked quickly in very high heat. Tandoori cooking adapts well to our barbecues.

The fillets are the small pieces on the underside of the breast. They make a great lead-in for a light dinner entrée.

Hush PUPPIES
with OKRA

Bet you can't eat only one. These cornmeal treats are popular with barbecue in Cajun country. They are served at room temperature, which means you can cook them well before your main course.

It's traditional—but optional—to stir a tablespoon of bacon drippings into the dough after the other ingredients have been mixed. If you don't keep bacon drippings, make a BLT for lunch and save some.

1 1/2 cups	yellow cornmeal
1 cup	flour
1 tsp	baking powder
1 tsp	salt
3/4 cup	buttermilk
2	large eggs, beaten
2	small onions, coarsely grated
4	large okra pods, minced
	oil for deep frying

Combine the cornmeal, flour, baking powder and salt in a large bowl. Make a well in the centre of these ingredients. Stir in the buttermilk and eggs, mixing the dough well. Mix the onions and okra into the dough, which should be stiff enough to hold its shape. If it is too thick, add a little more buttermilk.

In a deep fryer or a large frying pan, heat oil to 375°F. The oil should be at least 2 inches deep.

Use a spoon to scoop walnut-sized portions of the dough. Dip the spoon in oil from to time to make this easier. Drop the spoonfuls of dough into the hot oil and fry until golden brown on all sides. The hush puppies will puff up to the size of a small egg.

Yields 12 to 16

Jalapeño corn muffins

½ cup	fine cornmeal
½ cup	all-purpose flour
2 tsp	baking powder
1 ½ tsp	sugar
½ tsp	salt
1	large egg
½ cup	buttermilk
1 cup	cream-style corn
3 tbsp	butter, melted
2	medium jalapeño peppers, seeded and minced
	butter for greasing

In some European countries, cornmeal is a staple baking ingredient but is never combined with jalapeño peppers as it is in the southern United States, where corn muffins like these are a hit.

Preheat oven to 425°F.

Grease a 12-space muffin tin with butter and set aside.

If your cornmeal is coarse, put it into a blender and process it until it is fine before measuring it. Sift the cornmeal, flour, baking powder, sugar and salt into a large bowl.

Beat the egg. Add to the buttermilk and mix well. Stir in the corn, melted butter and jalapeño pepper.

Add the wet mixture to the dry, mixing thoroughly but gently. Spoon the cornmeal mixture into the muffin tin, filling each space about three-quarters full. Bake in the oven for 20 minutes until the tops are golden brown.

Allow to cool for 5 minutes. Remove and cool on cookie racks until room temperature.

Yields 10 to 12

Mushroom caps
with CILANTRO

If you think stuffed mushrooms have to have meat, discard the mushroom stems and replace them with minced prosciutto (¼ cup).

12	large mushrooms
4 tbsp	fine bread crumbs
1 tbsp	minced fresh cilantro
¼ tbsp	oregano powder
¼ tbsp	black pepper
⅛ tsp	salt
	olive oil
	sweet hot sauce (e.g., Tiger Sauce)

Clean the mushrooms and remove their stems. Mince the stems and put them into a bowl with the bread crumbs, cilantro, oregano, black pepper and salt. Toss the ingredients and add olive oil a little at a time until you get a thick paste.

Stuff the mushroom caps with this mixture, pressing it in well. Put a dab of hot sauce on top.

Preheat the barbecue to 400 to 450°F.

Arrange the caps on the unfired section of the barbecue and cook at high heat for 20 to 30 minutes.

Serves 4

Iced OYSTERS

16 small oysters, in the shell
      crushed ice
      sea salt
 2 large limes, each cut into 8 wedges
      Tabasco sauce

There is no recipe for oysters that beats this simple treatment. I think eating oysters raw is the best way to experience the flavour of these mineral-rich bivalves.

Arrange a layer of ice in 4 individual serving dishes. Shuck the oysters, leaving them in the bottom shell. Nestle 4 into each serving dish and refrigerate for 10 minutes.

Place the sea salt and Tabasco sauce on the table. Garnish each plate with 4 lime wedges and serve.

To eat: Sprinkle an oyster with sea salt, squeeze the juice of a lime wedge over the top, add a drop of Tabasco and enjoy real flavour.

Serves 4

Grilled OYSTERS
with oyster sauce

This Asian-style appetizer would be an impressive opener for any main course prepared in your backyard.

12 medium oysters, scrubbed clean
1/4 cup fresh lime juice
2 tbsp sugar
1 tbsp oyster sauce
1 tbsp soy sauce
1/4 tsp dried and crushed red chilies

Combine lime juice, sugar, oyster sauce, soy sauce and red chilies in a bowl and mix well.

Have the barbecue at a medium to high heat (350 to 400°F). Place the oysters over direct heat with the deep sides of their shells down. Close the lid and cook until the shells open. Wearing oven mitts, you should be able to remove the top shells and discard them.

Drizzle some of the prepared sauce over each oyster, close the lid and cook for 3 minutes more.

With oven mitts remove the oysters. Arrange them on individual dishes. Serve immediately.

Serves 4

Prawns
and CHICKEN TENDERS

12	large prawns, shells removed, tails left on
12	small chicken tenders
1/4 cup	fresh lime juice
	salt and pepper
1/2 cup	Spicy Dipping Sauce (page 25)
4	bamboo skewers

Soak the bamboo skewers in cold water for 30 minutes.

Run the skewers through the prawns and chicken tenders lengthwise, putting 3 prawns and 3 tenders on each skewer.

Grill directly over high heat (450° F) for 3 or 4 minutes. Turn and baste with the lime juice the entire cooking time.

Arrange on a platter, sprinkle with salt and pepper and serve with Spicy Dipping Sauce.

Serves 4

The small, separable oval of flesh on the underside of a chicken breast is the perfect size for this treatment. I call that piece of chicken a tender. Some butchers sell it as a chicken fillet.

PRAWNS chilled in a BELL PEPPER marinade

I made this dish originally without cooking the prawns. When I found that turned people off, I decided to steam them, which makes only a slight change in their texture. Be sure to keep the cooking time brief so the prawns retain all their flavour. Allow at least 4 hours for marinating.

8	large fresh prawns
1/2 cup	chopped roasted red bell peppers (see page 158)
1	medium vine-ripened tomato, chopped
2	large garlic cloves, chopped
2 tbsp	olive oil
2 tbsp	hot sauce (e.g., Melinda's XXXtra Hot Sauce)
2 tbsp	fresh lime juice
1/2 tsp	cumin powder
1/2 tsp	coriander powder
1	small butter lettuce
	baguette bread

Steam the prawns for only 1 minute, remove from the steamer and immerse in ice-cold water.

Whirl the roasted peppers, tomato, garlic, olive oil, hot sauce, lime juice, cumin powder and coriander powder in a food processor until puréed.

Remove the shells from the prawns, but leave the tails on, and place in a non-reactive bowl. Pour the purée over top, cover with food wrap and refrigerate for 4 hours or overnight. Toss several times.

To serve: Lightly toast slices of bread. Place the lettuce leaves on a platter around a small bowl of the marinade for dipping. Arrange the prawns on top of the lettuce and serve with the toasted bread.

Serves 4

CHILLED tomato soup
with prosciutto

6	paper-thin slices prosciutto
8	large vine-ripened tomatoes
1	large roasted red bell pepper, chopped (see page 158)
1 cup	croutons, or ¼ fine bread crumbs
1	large garlic clove, chopped
2 tbsp	olive oil
	salt

Fry the prosciutto in a non-stick frying pan until it begins to curl and sizzle. Place on a cutting board and chop coarsely. Set aside in a bowl.

Coarsely chop the tomatoes, retaining the juices. Purée the tomatoes and their juice, the bell pepper, croutons (or bread crumbs), garlic and olive oil in a food processor or blender until smooth. This may have to be done in several batches.

Put the purée into a bowl and stir in salt to taste. Cover with food wrap and refrigerate until chilled.

To serve: Stir the soup, ladle into 4 individual soup bowls, and sprinkle with equal amounts of the sizzled prosciutto.

Serves 4

Cold soups such as this are popular throughout southern Spain and in parts of Mexico as a starter for a mixed grill. A cured ham called serrano is used, but I have replaced it with prosciutto, which is easier to find.

If you don't have croutons on hand, dry bread crumbs will serve just as well to thicken the soup.

Gazpacho

A great chilled soup to kick off a summertime barbecue meal. With gazpacho, you can delete certain ingredients and add others to achieve the flavour you enjoy, but vine-ripened tomatoes are essential.

Make this a day ahead to allow the flavours to develop.

4	large vine-ripened tomatoes
1	medium zucchini
1	small yellow bell pepper
⅓ cup	chopped white onion
½ tbsp	coriander powder
½ tbsp	oregano powder
½ tbsp	salt
½ tsp	cumin powder
½ tsp	hot sauce (e.g., Melinda's XXXtra Hot Sauce)

Coarsely chop the tomatoes over a bowl so that you retain all the juices. Peel and seed the zucchini (scrape the seeds out with a spoon) and coarsely chop it. Seed the bell pepper and coarsely chop it. Put these vegetables, the chopped onion and the herbs and spices into a food processor and process off and on until the vegetables are finely chopped.

Refrigerate overnight but allow to stand at room temperature for an hour before serving.

Serves 4 to 6

BASTING AND DIPPING

sauces

MOST BASIC barbecue SAUCE

*As the name sug-
gests, this sauce is
basic and easy to
prepare. This recipe
makes enough to
baste on 1 serving of
meat or poultry for 4
people.*

1 cup   ketchup
2 tbsp   fresh lime juice
2 tbsp   Worcestershire sauce
2 tbsp   prepared mustard
1 tbsp   hot sauce (e.g., Melinda's XXXtra Hot Sauce)

Combine all the ingredients in a bowl and mix well. It's
ready to use.

Yields 1 cup

Lime BASTING SAUCE

2 cups	undiluted frozen limeade, thawed
1 cup	ketchup
1/2 cup	port
1/4 cup	grainy mustard
1 tbsp	salt
1 tsp	dried and crushed red chilies

Combine all the ingredients in a saucepan. Bring to a simmer and cook for 5 minutes. Remove from the heat and cool before using.

Leftover sauce can be kept in the refrigerator for up to 10 days.

Yields 3 1/2 cups

When travelling the back roads of Mexico, I've found roadside vendors grilling chicken pieces basted with a sauce similar to this. I have brushed it on meat and seafood, but chicken seems to be its better mate.

Mustard BARBECUE SAUCE

Fruit- and mustard-based barbecue sauces have become as popular as traditional tomato-based sauces. This was inspired by one I ate in Arizona. I recommend it for chicken thighs and pork.

2 cups	grainy mustard
2 cups	cider vinegar
1 cup	prepared mustard
½ cup	demerara sugar
2 tbsp	fresh lime juice
2 tbsp	Worcestershire sauce
2 tbsp	hot sauce (e.g., Tabasco)

Combine all the ingredients in a saucepan. Cook over low heat until the sugar has dissolved. Continue to simmer over very low heat, without a lid for about 10 minutes until the sauce has thickened. Allow to cool before using.

Yields 4 cups

ORANGE barbecue sauce

2 cups	undiluted frozen orange juice, thawed
1/2 cup	port
2 tbsp	hot sauce (e.g., Tabasco)
1 tsp	cumin powder

Combine all the ingredients and mix well. Brush the sauce on meat or seafood in the last 4 or 5 minutes of cooking. The sugar in the orange juice and port tends to caramelize if you baste too soon.

Yields 2 1/2 cups

This is a fruity barbecue sauce with a slight bite to it. If you want to moderate the bite, omit the hot sauce and add the equivalent amount of water. This sauce is a good match with meat and seafood.

Rum and papaya
barbecue
sauce

This recipe has fewer ingredients than any other barbecue sauce I use, but these are all you need to add a pleasing fruit flavour to grilled meat and seafood.

3 large papayas
¼ cup dark rum
¼ cup undiluted frozen orange juice, thawed

Peel and seed the papaya. Coarsely chop the fruit and put it into a food processor or blender. Add the rum and orange juice and process until smooth and slightly runny. If needed, add more rum, a little at a time.

Baste with this in the final 5 minutes of grilling.

Yields enough for 1 use

Sweet and sour barbecue sauce

1 cup	ketchup
½ cup	vinegar
½ cup	water
½ cup	demerara sugar
2 tbsp	hot sauce (e.g., Melinda's XXXtra Hot Sauce)

Combine all the ingredients in a saucepan and cook over a high heat, only until the sugar has dissolved. Remove from the heat and cool before using.

Yields 2½ cups

This will probably remind you of the first North American Chinese food you ever ate. When grilling pork, chicken or shrimp with this sauce, baste in the last few minutes of cooking to avoid burning the sugar. Pass extra sauce at the table.

Chimichurri dipping sauce

The essential ingredients in this Argentinian sauce are parsley, garlic, hot pepper, herbs, oil and vinegar, but many variations exist. Here is mine.

Chimichurri sauce is served with beef.

1/2 cup	olive oil
2 tbsp	cider vinegar
1 tbsp	raspberry vinegar
1/2 cup	minced parsley
8	large garlic cloves, minced
1 tsp	oregano powder
1/4 tsp	cayenne pepper
1/4 tsp	salt

Combine all the ingredients in a jar and mix well. Cover with a lid and allow to stand at room temperature for 4 to 6 hours before using. Shake several times.

Yields enough for 1 use

Horseradish
SAUCE

¾ cup	mayonnaise
2 tbsp	medium-hot horseradish
⅓ cup	fresh lime juice
2 tbsp	Worcestershire sauce
1 tbsp	tomato paste
1 tbsp	grated onion
1 tsp	salt

This sauce is best when prepared 1 to 2 days in advance, allowing all the ingredients to meld. I usually serve it with beef from the grill.

Combine all the ingredients in a non-reactive bowl, cover and refrigerate until ready to serve.

Yields 1 cup

HOT pepper SAUCE

Here's a homemade sauce that could substitute for Melinda's XXXtra Hot Sauce. Try adding it to mayonnaise, increasing the quantity until you get the heat you like. Or dash a few drops into soups, chowders or rice.

1/2 cup	olive oil
6	large garlic cloves, minced
1/4 cup	cayenne pepper
3 tbsp	cumin powder
2 tbsp	white pepper
2 tbsp	paprika
2 tbsp	coriander powder
1 tsp	salt

Combine the cayenne, cumin, white pepper, paprika, coriander and salt in a jar, mixing them well. Add the olive oil and garlic, again mixing all the ingredients well. You should have about 1/4 inch of olive oil over the other ingredients.

Screw the lid tightly on the jar and refrigerate. Shake before using. The sauce will keep under refrigeration for about 2 weeks.

Yields 3/4 cup

Lime
MAYONNAISE

2 large egg yolks (see page 158)
2 tbsp fresh lime juice
2 tbsp Dijon mustard
½ tsp sugar
1½ cups olive oil

Process the egg yolks, lime juice, mustard and sugar in a food processor or blender. With the unit still running, slowly add the olive oil and process until the mixture becomes thick and creamy.

Yields 2 cups

About 3 times a week during the summer, I whip up a batch of this mayo and use it on hamburgers, sandwiches or sausages.

I've never worried about eating uncooked eggs, but because there can be reason for concern, I give two methods for pasteurizing raw eggs.

Red velvet SAUCE

You can buy roasted red bell peppers or roast your own. You will need 3 big peppers to make the 2 cups called for here. Also, check out the instructions for dealing with raw eggs.

You can buy roasted red bell peppers or roast your own. You will need 3 big peppers to make the 2 cups called for here. Also, check out the instructions for dealing with raw eggs.

This is a colourful, tangy sauce for pork.

2 cups	chopped roasted red bell peppers (see page 158)
1 cup	olive oil, divided
4 tbsp	sweet hot sauce (e.g., Tiger Sauce)
2 tbsp	fresh lime juice
1 tbsp	grainy mustard
1	large egg (see page 158)
1 tsp	black pepper
1/2 tsp	salt

Put 1/2 cup of the olive oil, the hot sauce, lime juice, mustard, egg, and pepper and salt in a food processor and process for 3 to 5 seconds.

With the appliance running, drizzle the remaining olive oil into the mixture until it thickens to about the consistency of mayonnaise.

Add the roasted pepper to the food processor and process on and off only until the peppers are coarsely chopped. Transfer to a bowl and serve at room temperature.

Yields 2 cups

Spicy dipping sauce

¾ cup	dark soy sauce
¼ cup	liquid honey
2	large garlic cloves, minced
1 tbsp	dried and crushed red chilies
1½ tbsp	mustard flour
	cold water

A quickie with a bite. Great for dipping meats or vegetables grilled on skewers.

Combine the soy sauce, honey, garlic and red chilies in a small saucepan and bring to a very low simmer.

Place the mustard flour in a bowl. Stir in just enough water to produce a runny paste and blend it into the soy sauce mixture.

Transfer to a bowl and allow to cool to room temperature before serving.

Yields 1 cup

Thousand Island
sauce

This is a simple version of the classic dressing. Not only can it be used as a salad dressing, but it will also give burgers or hot dogs zing.

1 cup	mayonnaise
1/3 cup	bottled chili sauce
1 tbsp	fresh lime juice
1/4 cup	minced green onion
2 tbsp	minced sweet pickles
1/2 tsp	paprika
1/4 tsp	cayenne pepper
1	large egg, hard-boiled and grated

Combine the mayonnaise, chili sauce and lime juice. Add the remaining ingredients, stirring the dressing well.

Under refrigeration, this dressing will keep for 4 or 5 days.

Yields 1 1/2 cups

RUBS AND Marinades

Rubs come in two forms: dry and wet. Both are intended to add flavour, not to tenderize. Dry rubs are concocted from dry or dehydrated ingredients, salt, sugar, pepper and a great variety of herbs and spices. What I call a sprinkle is essentially a mixture of similar dry ingredients, but it's used like salt and pepper rather than being rubbed into the meat. Wet rubs contain dry herbs and spices but also have garlic and possibly oil or butter.

I make up wet rubs for immediate use, but I store my dry rubs in the freezer. Resealable plastic bags are good for this.

My preference is to marinate most dishes overnight. That's simply the way I work: I begin to prepare food ahead for eating on the following day. It's my belief, however, that a shorter period of marinating at room temperature accomplishes about the same as a longer period under refrigeration. With these marinades, you can usually choose the longer or shorter period.

My goal with marinating meat or poultry is to add flavour. Marinating fish also adds flavour or sometimes overcomes strong unattractive flavours. Some fish when marinated become firmer and stand up better to handling on the barbecue.

Cajun
SPRINKLE

2 tbsp	paprika
2 tbsp	black pepper
1 tbsp	garlic salt
1 tbsp	onion salt
1 tbsp	white pepper
1/2 tsp	cayenne pepper

Combine all the ingredients and mix well. Sprinkle the desired amount over the meat before cooking.

The paprika in this sprinkle gives a nice colour, but because it is absorbent, it also retains juices and keeps meat or poultry more moist. Use this as you would salt and pepper before cooking.

CURRY sprinkle

Curry isn't a standard barbecue flavour, but we all have different tastes. If you like Indian cooking and want a change, give it a try.

2 tbsp	curry powder
1 tbsp	coriander powder
1 tbsp	cumin powder
1 tbsp	black pepper
½ tbsp	garlic powder
½ tbsp	onion powder
1 tsp	salt

Combine all the ingredients and mix well. Sprinkle on chicken and shrimp and allow to stand for 15 minutes before grilling.

Garlic HOTsauce RUB

12	large garlic cloves, minced
1/4 cup	hot sauce (e.g., Melinda's XXXtra Hot Sauce)
2 tbsp	grainy mustard
1 tbsp	cumin powder
1 tbsp	coriander powder
1/2 tbsp	black pepper

The garlic cloves make this a wet rub which I use exclusively on cuts of beef that take a longer cooking time, such as roasts or thick slabs of steak.

Combine all the ingredients, mixing them very well. Rub the mixture all over a piece of beef and allow to stand at room temperature for 30 minutes before cooking.

Salt and **pepper** RUB

The only black pepper I use is Tellicherry. Although I don't specify it for many recipes, I recommend it for this rub. It is more complex than other black peppers. If you can't find it in your supermarket, use regular ground black pepper. Lawry's is the seasoned salt and pepper I buy.

2 tbsp   onion salt
2 tbsp   garlic salt
2 tbsp   seasoned salt
2 tbsp   lemon pepper
1 tbsp   seasoned black pepper
2 tbsp   black pepper

Combine all the ingredients in a bowl and mix well. Sprinkle the rub liberally over an entire roast, rub it in with your fingers and allow to stand at room temperature for 30 minutes before cooking.

Poultry
RUB

2 tbsp   savory
2 tbsp   lemon pepper
2 tbsp   paprika
1 tsp   garlic powder
1 tsp   onion powder
2 tbsp   salt

Combine all the ingredients and mix well. Sprinkle over poultry, rub in with your fingers and let sit for 10 or 15 minutes before cooking.

Savory is an herb we associate with turkey dressing and festive meals. You can add that holiday flavour to chicken, turkey or Cornish game hens with this rub. Put it on skinned poultry or if you are leaving the skin on, rub some into the skin and slip some under it.

PAT'S winning RUB

About 1990, Pat decided that if she was going to be up with me all night cooking for a barbecue competition, she might as well enter the event herself. To create her own rub, she added pineapple jello powder to the Simple Texas Rub. Of course I laughed, but apparently the judges enjoyed the sweetness of her creation because Pat won the event.

1 cup   Simple Texas Rub (see next page)
½ cup   pineapple jello powder

Combine the ingredients and mix well. Rub vigorously into the meat and allow to stand for 30 minutes before cooking.

SIMPLE Texas RUB

1 cup black pepper
1 cup paprika
1 cup chili powder
½ cup salt

Combine all the ingredients and mix well. Rub a generous amount on meat and leave for 20 minutes or longer before cooking.

While I put this on pork cutlets, Texans would use it only on beef. In fact, until about 10 years ago, Texans never barbecued anything but beef. Now, because of competitions, they include pork in their outdoor cooking at home.

Tandoori RUB

This Indian-style rub is usually reserved for chicken, but also goes well with pork. It has quite a kick. To tone it down, cut back on the white pepper.

3 tbsp	curry powder
1 tbsp	white pepper
1 tbsp	ginger powder
1 tbsp	paprika
1 tsp	coriander powder
1 tsp	nutmeg

Combine all the ingredients and mix well. When using, rub well into the meat and allow to stand for 20 minutes before grilling.

Fish marinade GLAZE

¹/₄ cup   mayonnaise
3 tbsp   fresh lime juice
2 tbsp   grainy mustard
1 tbsp   seasoned salt

Combine all the ingredients and mix well. Spread the marinade over the entire fish fillet, which can marinate in the refrigerator overnight or stand for 30 minutes at room temperature before grilling.

Because of the mayonnaise, this marinade also clings like a glaze. The mixture works well on salmon fillets and most white fish. This will make enough to cover a 2- to 3-pound salmon fillet.

MARINADE teriyaki

This is a basic marinade to produce that Japanese flavour. I usually dip chicken and beef into this one, but go ahead and try it with pork or prawns.

¾ cup   soy sauce
½ cup   port
½ cup   demerara sugar
¼ cup   cider vinegar
¼ cup   olive oil
2 tbsp   grated fresh ginger

Combine the ingredients in a saucepan and cook over low heat just long enough to dissolve the sugar. Remove from the heat and allow to cool before using.

Mexican marinade

½ cup	fresh minced cilantro
¼ cup	olive oil
¼ cup	fresh lime juice
3	large garlic cloves, minced
2 tsp	hot sauce (e.g., Melinda's XXXtra Hot Sauce)
2 tsp	dried Mexican oregano
½ tsp	salt

Combine all the ingredients in a non-reactive bowl and mix well. Marinate any seafood for 30 minutes to an hour only. Baste with the marinade during the grilling time.

I gave this the Mexican handle because of the large amount of cilantro. Its refreshing taste makes it different from other marinades. I find it not assertive enough for beef, but enhancing for seafood, especially shrimp, prawns and white fish.

PORT marinade

This is one is good for wild game, but I have used it success- fully in competitions when barbecuing lamb and basting chicken kebabs.

¾ cup   port
½ cup   olive oil
¼ cup   soy sauce
2 tbsp   garlic powder
2 tbsp   onion powder
1 tbsp   black pepper

Combine all the ingredients in a saucepan and bring to a low simmer. Cook for 10 minutes to blend the ingredients. Cool before using.

Spicy hoisin MARINADE

¼ cup	hoisin sauce
3 tbsp	fresh lime juice
2 tbsp	sugar
2 tbsp	hot sauce (e.g., Melinda's XXXtra Hot Sauce)

Combine the ingredients and mix well. As a marinade, use it for short marinating periods, from 30 minutes to an hour.

This marinade works well with all meats and many seafoods but has its best effect on poultry and pork. It could also be a basting or dipping sauce. Remember that a mixture cannot do double duty as marinade and dipping sauce unless it has been cooked.

WILD game marinade

Most people want to marinate wild game meats to moderate any noticeable gamy taste. This marinade also works well with strong-tasting fish, such as swordfish, tuna and mackerel.

½ cup cola beverage (flat)
½ cup port
¼ cup fresh lime juice
¼ cup soy sauce
2 tbsp sugar

Combine all the ingredients in a container with a tight-fitting lid and shake until the sugar is dissolved. Let fish or game marinate in this mixture for at least 6 hours or overnight.

Beef

Beef has got to be the number-one choice for barbecue cooking. Most people light up the barbecue with the idea of quickly grilling a steak or hamburger. This chapter focuses on grilling, using a variety of treatments for the more tender cuts of beef.

People ask me why I'm always flavouring my grilled steaks with herbs and spices. The reason is that tender beef is not as tasty as the well-used muscles that give us chuck roasts or briskets.

The choicest cuts of beef come from the short loin. Within the short loin is a large, long, tapering muscle called the tenderloin, which is often cut into steaks. Many of the flavour treatments I've developed for grilled beef call for tenderloin steaks, which I think should be cooked either rare or medium-rare.

A steak that combines both tenderness and flavour is the porterhouse, which is cut from the thick end of the short loin towards the cow's well-exercised hindquarter. I also grill sirloin steaks from the hindquarter, and rib-eyes from the section forward of the short loin. Both are tasty, tender cuts of meat.

Whatever cut of beef you are buying, the meat should be smooth, close-grained and bright red. The fat should be white and firm.

Not just a
BURGER

1¼ lbs	lean ground beef
1 tsp	black pepper
2 tbsp	olive oil
1	medium red onion
1	medium red bell pepper, seeds removed
4	large plum tomatoes, coarsely chopped
2	large garlic cloves, minced
2 tbsp	capers, chopped
1 tsp	coriander powder
1 tsp	salt
½ tsp	oregano powder
½ tsp	dried and crushed red chilies
	Kaiser buns, halved
	butter

The beef pattie is standard, but the cooked vegetable topping makes this recipe special. There's no need for ketchup and mustard to give this hamburger great flavour.

Cut the onion and bell pepper into thin slices. Heat the olive oil in a non-stick frying pan over medium to high heat. Add the onion and cook until the slices begin to brown lightly. Add the bell pepper slices and cook until they are limp. Add the tomatoes, garlic, capers, coriander, salt, oregano and red chilies, cooking for 3 minutes more. Remove from the heat and keep at room temperature.

Combine the ground beef and black pepper, mixing them well. Shape into 4 equal patties and grill directly over medium to high heat (350 to 400 °F). Cook for about 6 minutes a side until they just begin to char. Turn the patties often.

When the meat is nearly cooked, place the buns (cut side down) on the grill, lightly toast them and slather with butter.

Put a meat pattie on the bottom half of a bun and distribute some topping over each. Cover with the top of the bun and serve.

Serves 4

A perfect hamburger
with lime mayonnaise

Having eaten hamburgers at a variety of fast-food chains, we've probably all realized that if we want a great burger, we should prepare it ourselves.

If you haven't time to make the Lime Mayonnaise, you could stir some lime juice to your taste into a commercial mayo.

1 lb	lean ground beef
¼ cup	minced green onions, green ends only
¼ cup	barbecue sauce (e.g., The Fire Chef)
¼ cup	fine bread crumbs
1	medium egg
4	medium Kaiser buns, halved
¼ cup	Lime Mayonnaise (page 23)
	butter
4	slices vine-ripened tomatoes (¼ inch thick)
4	slices red onion (⅛ inch thick)

Combine the ground beef, green onions, barbecue sauce and bread crumbs in a bowl. Mix by hand. Add the egg and mix it into the meat. Shape into 4 patties about 5 inches round.

Grill the patties directly over medium to high heat (350 to 400°F) until the insides are medium to well done and the outsides are lightly charred.

When the meat is nearly done, grill the Kaiser buns lightly. Apply butter to the top half and equal amounts of the lime mayonnaise to the bottom half. Build the hamburgers with meat patties and tomato and onion slices.

Serves 4

NEW YORK STEAK
with bourbon

2   New York steaks (12 oz each)
1 cup   bourbon
¾ cup   brown sugar
½ cup   barbecue sauce (e.g., The Fire Chef)

Cook the bourbon and brown sugar in a saucepan over low heat just long enough to melt the sugar. Remove and allow to cool.

Arrange the steaks in a dish, pour the bourbon mixture over top and marinate for 30 minutes, turning the steaks several times. Remove the steaks and pat dry with a paper towel. Mix the barbecue sauce into the bourbon mixture.

Dip the steaks into the sauce and grill directly over high heat (400 to 450°F) until done to your preference (5 to 6 minutes for rare, 8 for medium). Turn the steaks often and baste with the sauce several times.

Because of the sugar in the sauce, the steaks should be well charred on the outside but medium to rare on the inside.

Serves 2

New York steaks, sometimes sold as strip loin, are among the most popular cuts grilled on the barbecue. They are lean and very flavourful, but this short marinating boosts the flavour quotient.

Because of the brown sugar and the sugar in the alcohol, you may experience a flare-up. Keep a spray bottle of water mixed with baking soda to squelch the flame or turn off the gas and move the meat to another part of the grill until the flame dies.

Peppercorn
HERB steaks

In restaurants, peppercorn steaks are seared on a heavy metal grill or frying pan. The pepper burns and you perceive a heavy, pungent flavour. Done my way, you can still taste the fresh peppercorns and all the herbs.

2	New York steaks (¾ inch thick)
1 tbsp	green peppercorns
1 tbsp	white peppercorns
1 tsp	dried sage
1 tsp	dried basil leaves
1 tsp	dried and crushed rosemary
1 tsp	celery salt
	olive oil

Coarsely crush the peppercorns and combine with the sage, basil, rosemary and celery salt. Mix well and apply to both sides of the steaks, pressing the crushed peppercorns in firmly.

Grill the steaks directly over high heat (400°F) for about 6 minutes a side, turning and basting lightly with the olive oil. This will give you a rare steak. For medium, add 3 minutes a side.

Serves 2

Carne asada
(Mexican steak)

4	New York steaks (¹/₂ inch thick)
1 tbsp	fajita seasoning (e.g., Spice Island)
	olive oil

Remove all the fat from the outer edge of the steaks and discard.

With the blunt edge of a large knife, pound the steaks on both sides, breaking down the fibers. Sprinkle both sides of the meat with the fajita seasoning, using it all.

Place the steaks in a dish in one layer. Drizzle with olive oil and allow to stand at room temperature for 30 minutes, turning several times in the oil.

Grill the steaks directly over medium to high heat (350 to 400°F) for 4 minutes a side, turning several times and basting with the olive oil in which the steaks marinated, using all the oil.

Serves 4

If you order carne asada in a small town in Mexico, you usually get a tough steak. It may be fairly thin, but still hard to chew. When I grill a steak in this Mexican-inspired style, I choose a thin New York steak, which I know will be tender.

Basting with oil as you grill will give the steaks the authentic oily appearance of carne asada.

Porterhouse
steak

Here it is: the tender steak with that full beef taste. No need of herbs or spices. Let it come to room temperature and then grill it. Simple, but true to the beef and for 2 people with big appetites. With the bone in, the steaks will weigh more than a pound each.

2   porterhouse steaks (1 inch thick)
     salt and pepper

Sprinkle the steaks with salt and pepper and grill directly over medium to high heat (350 to 400 °F) turning often. For a rare steak, grill for 8 minutes a side. For medium, go for 3 minutes extra on each side.

Serves 2 (big eaters)

RIB-EYE steps
with bell peppers

4	bone-in rib-eye steaks (10 oz each)
¼ cup	chili powder
2 tbsp	black pepper
1 tbsp	celery salt
4	medium red bell peppers
	salt

The beef on the ribs is often rolled into a roast, but it can also be cut into steaks. In the past few years rib-eyes have become one of the more popular barbecue steaks. Grilled bell peppers go well with them.

Remove the stems from the tops and seeds from the insides of the peppers. Sprinkle the insides with salt and set aside on paper towels, with the tops down.

Combine the chili powder, black pepper and celery salt and mix well. Rub the mixture over the steaks, using it all. Put the steaks on a dish and hold at room temperature for 30 minutes.

Grill the peppers directly over medium heat (350°F) until they become very limp and just begin to char. Turn often during the cooking period. Gently remove from the barbecue, making sure they remain whole. Place in a resealable plastic bag, seal and set aside.

Grill the steaks directly over medium to high heat (350 to 400°F.) for about 12 minutes, turning the steaks often. This will produce a medium to rare steak.

Turn the heat to high (450°F). Gently return the peppers to the barbecue. Lightly char the steaks and peppers; this will take only 2 to 3 minutes.

Place steaks on individual dinner plates, arrange a grilled pepper on the side and sprinkle lightly with salt before serving.

Serves 4

Texas beef ribs
with sweet sauce

Every time I've been in Texas, I've seen people barbecue beef ribs with a very sweet sauce like this one. You'll need lots of damp napkins to wipe off sticky fingers.

Although this isn't the fastest recipe, the ribs need only a quick sprinkle of seasoning before they go on the barbecue where you can ignore them for an hour while preparing and simmering a glaze. The final grilling and glazing will take 30 to 45 minutes.

2	racks beef side ribs
2 tbsp	celery salt
2 tbsp	black pepper
2 cups	ketchup
½ cup	molasses
½ cup	apple juice
1 tbsp	coriander powder

Preheat the barbecue to 300°F.

Sprinkle the ribs with a tablespoon of celery salt and black pepper and put them on the unfired area of the barbecue and cook for 1 hour at medium heat.

Combine the remaining ingredients in a saucepan and bring to a boil. Lower the heat and simmer until the mixture becomes very thick, stirring often. This will take 30 to 45 minutes.

Raise the heat in the barbecue to 350°F. Keep the ribs on the unfired area and begin to apply the glaze, brushing it on liberally to both sides of the ribs. Barbecue until the ribs are well browned and thickly glazed with the sauce. This will take 30 to 45 minutes.

Serves 4

Skewered Oysters with Yogurt Curry Dipping Sauce, p. 106

STUFFED
sirloin steak

1	top sirloin steak (3 lbs, 2 inches thick)
1 tbsp	olive oil
1 cup	chopped green onions
8	large garlic cloves, minced
1/4 cup	fine bread crumbs
3 tbsp	sweet hot sauce (e.g., Tiger Sauce)
1 tbsp	black pepper
1/2 tsp	salt
	olive oil

If you stuff the steak earlier in the day, it will take only 30 minutes to get this impressive dish on the table.

To save yourself some time, have your butcher trim all the fat off the steak and cut the pocket for you.

To prepare the stuffing, heat the olive oil in a small frying pan. Sauté the green onions for 3 minutes, stir in the garlic and sauté for 2 minutes more. Remove from the heat, blend in the bread crumbs, sweet hot sauce, pepper and salt.

Cut a pocket in the steak, making a horizontal cut through the centre, parallel to the top surface, stopping the cut about 1 inch from each side and from the opposite end.

Fill the pocket with the stuffing. Secure the open end with small skewers or sew shut with butcher's twine.

Grill the steak directly over medium to high heat (350 to 400°F) for approximately 10 to 12 minutes a side. Turn and baste often with the olive oil.

Raise the heat to high (450°F) and cook the steak a little longer to slightly char it.

Transfer to a large cutting board and remove the skewers or twine. Carve into 1/2-inch slices and serve.

Serves 4 to 6

Leg of Lamb with a Bread-Crumb Crust, p.78

Mediterranean STEAK

This is one of the few recipes in which I grill a less tender steak to take advantage of the more intense beef flavour Europeans prefer. I've also created a Mediterranean taste with the oregano and Parmesan. This steak won't melt in your mouth, but it's yummy.

4	sirloin steaks (8 oz each, 1/2 inch thick)
6	large garlic cloves
1/8 tsp	salt
1 tbsp	dried and crushed oregano
1/2 tsp	black pepper
3/4 cup	olive oil
	freshly grated Parmesan

Peel and mince the garlic. Sprinkle with the salt and mash with the flat of a large knife.

Combine the mashed garlic, oregano and black pepper and rub well into both sides of the steaks. Place in a dish in one layer and drizzle the olive oil over top. Allow to stand at room temperature for 20 minutes, gently turning the steaks several times.

Grill the steaks directly over high heat (400 to 450°F) for 4 minutes a side, turning and basting several times with the olive oil and garlic mixture. Sprinkle liberally with the Parmesan and cook for 3 minutes more.

Serves 4

Coriander-spiced **tenderloin steaks**

4	beef tenderloin steaks (6 oz each, ¾ inch thick)
1 tsp	black pepper
1 tsp	cumin powder
1 tsp	coriander powder
1 tsp	sugar
½ tsp	celery salt
½ tsp	garlic salt
¼ tsp	white pepper

Choice cuts of beef, such as these steaks from the tenderloin, are generally less flavourful than the tougher cuts. They need a little enhancement, which this spice mixture provides.

Combine all the spices and rub both sides of the steaks with the mixture. Allow to stand at room temperature for 15 to 30 minutes before cooking.

Grill the steaks directly over medium to high heat (350 to 400 °F), turning several times until done to your preference. For rare, grill about 6 minutes a side. For medium, increase the cooking time by 3 minutes on each side.

Serves 4

Tenderloin steaks
with a ginger sauce

I've taken one of my favourite Asian wok dishes and adapted it for the barbecue.

You can replace the beef tenderloin with a less tender cut of beef, such as a New York steak, but you will have to lengthen the marinating time to an hour.

Serve over a bed of rice noodles along with a green salad.

4   beef tenderloin steaks (6 oz each, ¾ inch thick)
¼ cup   light soy sauce
3 tbsp   cider vinegar
2 tbsp   olive oil
2 tbsp   grated fresh ginger
2   large garlic cloves, minced

Place the steaks in a shallow dish. Put the soy sauce, cider vinegar, oil, ginger and garlic into a blender and process until smooth. Pour this mixture over the steaks and marinate at room temperature for 30 minutes. Turn the steaks several times.

Grill the steaks directly over medium to high heat (350 to 400°F) for about 6 minutes a side for rare, turning the steaks often. Continue grilling for 3 minutes more a side for a medium steak.

While the steaks are grilling, pour the marinade into a small saucepan. Bring to a boil and simmer until reduced by half.

Arrange the steaks over rice noodles. Ladle some of the sauce over each steak before serving.

Serves 4

Open-faced
steak sandwich
WITH ROASTED GARLIC

4	beef tenderloin steaks (6 oz each, ¾ inch thick)
4	slices French bread, lightly toasted
4 tbsp	roasted garlic (see page 158)
4	large slices tomato (½ inch thick)
½ cup	minced oil-packed dried tomatoes
1 tbsp	grainy Dijon mustard
2 tsp	olive oil
	coarse sea salt

This is a knife-and-fork sandwich, the ultimate casual treatment of a fancy steak. If you have prepared the roasted garlic and have salad greens ready to coat with a dressing, you can have dinner on the table in 10 minutes.

Mix the minced dried tomatoes, Dijon mustard and olive oil in a small bowl and bring to the barbecue, along with the roasted garlic.

Lightly toast the slices of bread on the barbecue, spread the garlic paste equally on all 4 and set aside.

Grill the steaks and tomato slices directly over high heat (400 to 450°F) for 4 minutes a side. Remove the steaks and tomato slices from the grill and lower the heat to medium and shut off all but one burner.

Put a steak on each slice of toasted bread with a slice of tomato on top. Ladle equal amounts of the dried tomato, mustard and oil mixture on the tomato. Return the sandwiches to the unfired area of the barbecue and close the lid. Barbecue for 2 minutes more for a medium-rare steak. Put the sandwiches on individual dinner plates and sprinkle with coarse sea salt before serving.

Serves 2

Tenderloin steaks with
asiago

4	beef tenderloin steaks, (6 oz each, ¾ inch thick)
2	large plum tomatoes
¼ cup	crumbled asiago
½ tsp	dried and crushed oregano
	olive oil

Peel and seed the tomatoes and squeeze all the juice from them. Chop the tomatoes and add them to the crumbled asiago.

Rub the steaks with the oregano and grill directly over medium to high (350 to 400°F) for about 6 minutes a side, turning and basting with the olive oil often.

Move the steaks to the unfired area of the barbecue. Spread some cheese mixture over top of each steak and cook for 5 minutes longer. This should produce a medium-well-done steak.

Serves 4

TEQUILA STEAKS
with cilantro

4	beef tenderloin steaks (6 oz each, ¾ inch thick)
2 tbsp	tequila
2 tbsp	olive oil
2	large garlic cloves, minced
¼ cup	butter
¼ cup	chopped fresh cilantro

Tequila has a unique flavour. Don't try to find a substitute and don't add salt and pepper, which just aren't necessary.

Place the steaks in a small dish in one layer. Combine the tequila, olive oil and garlic, mix well and pour over the steaks. Allow them to stand at room temperature for 20 minutes, turning several times.

Soften the butter in a small saucepan, stir in the cilantro and set aside.

Grill the steaks directly over high heat (400 to 450°F) for about 5 minutes a side, turning often and basting with the tequila marinade. The steaks will be rare.

To serve, dot each steak with some of the cilantro butter.

Serves 4

Perri perri BEEF
and cantaloupe kebabs

1 lb	beef tenderloin
2	medium onions
1/2	large cantaloupe
4 tbsp	perri perri sauce
2 tbsp	liquid honey
2 tbsp	fresh lime juice
8	bamboo skewers

Soak the bamboo skewers in cold water.

To prepare the marinade, combine the perri perri sauce, honey and lime juice.

Cut the beef into 16 equal cubes and place in a shallow bowl. Pour the marinade over top, tossing the cubes to coat them with the marinade. Allow to stand at room temperature for 15 minutes, tossing several times.

In the meantime, skin and cut the onions into 12 wedges. Seed and peel the cantaloupe and cut it into 12 equal cubes.

Thread a cube of meat onto a skewer, followed by a wedge of onion and a cube of cantaloupe. Repeat this twice more and finish with another cube of meat. This will give you 4 kebabs. To keep the meat, onion and cantaloupe pieces from spinning, insert another skewer parallel to the first.

Grill the kebabs directly over medium to high heat (350 to 400°F) until the meat, onion and cantaloupe are slightly charred, basting with the marinade until it is all used. This should take about 8 minutes.

Serves 2

PORK AND Lamb

I n the years since I got into barbecuing, pork has changed. It's now leaner, with some cuts being as lean as chicken. If you use a low-fat cooking method (and barbecue is a low-fat method), three ounces of pork tenderloin has the same amount of fat as a roasted, skinless chicken breast.

The tenderloin is one of my favourite pork cuts. Sliced and pounded thin, medallions from the tenderloin can be grilled in minutes. Kept whole, the tenderloin benefits from the indirect barbecuing method which prevents it from drying out. Because the tenderloin usually weighs about three-quarters of a pound, it doesn't take long to barbecue off direct heat.

Most of the other pork cuts I use for grilling—the chops, steaks and butt roast—are lean. It's true that side ribs are higher in fat content, but my riblets recipe calls for meaty side ribs cut into thirds, reducing the fat content by a third. (Just ribbing you: What would barbecue be without some fat?)

Lamb marketing boards have also drawn up tables to show that their product is low in fat and cholesterol. If you can manage to eat only three ounces of topside Australian lamb, you'll be getting five grams of fat, slightly more than in the same amount of pork tenderloin or that roasted, skinless chicken breast.

Most people also grill lamb steaks and kebabs, which I enjoy too. But the leg of lamb isn't an obvious choice for quick cooking on the barbecue. If the meat of the leg is butterflied, it can be grilled over direct heat or barbecued off heat. I give recipes for both.

When you are shopping, look for pork that is light pink in colour with pure white fat. Lamb should be rosy pink with firm, white fat.

PORK CHOPS
with maple syrup

4	centre-cut pork chops (6 oz each)
½ cup	maple syrup
¼ cup	sweet hot sauce (e.g., Tiger Sauce)
2 tbsp	dark rum
1 tsp	dried and crushed red chilies
1 cup	Mushroom Compote (see page 117)

Using a wooden food mallet, pound the chops out to twice their size, making sure that you do not release the meat from the bone. Place in a shallow dish and set aside.

Combine and mix the maple syrup, hot sauce, rum and chilies. Pour over the chops. Marinate for 45 minutes at room temperature, turning the chops several times.

Remove the chops from the marinade and grill over high heat (425 to 500°F) for about 6 minutes a side, turning and basting often with the marinade.

Remove from the barbecue and place 2 chops on each dinner plate. Top each with ¼ cup of hot Mushroom Compote and serve.

Serves 2

If you like, have your butcher french the pork chops. All that means is cutting off the fatty piece of meat from the end of the bone, which you could probably do yourself. The rum in the marinade adds a Jamaican touch.

PORK ONLY kebabs

In the southwest United States, these vegetable-less kebabs are served with baked beans and a salad.

2 lbs	pork loin, outside fat removed
1 cup	hoisin sauce
1/4 cup	port
1/4 cup	tomato sauce
2 tbsp	Tabasco sauce
2 tbsp	crushed oregano
4	large garlic cloves, minced
	bamboo skewers

Soak the bamboo skewers in water for about 30 minutes.

Cut the pork into 1-inch cubes, thread onto skewers and place in a shallow dish.

Combine the hoisin sauce, port, tomato sauce, Tabasco sauce, oregano and garlic and mix well. Pour over the kebabs and allow to stand at room temperature for 30 minutes.

Grill the kebabs directly over medium to high heat (350 to 400°F) for 10 to 15 minutes, turning and basting with the marinade until the meat is brown all over.

Serves 4

Barbecue riblets with hoisin and black bean sauces

3 lbs	meaty pork side ribs
1/3 cup	hoisin sauce
3 tbsp	olive oil
2 tbsp	black bean sauce
2 tbsp	undiluted frozen orange juice, thawed
4	large garlic cloves, minced

Have your butcher cut the rack of ribs lengthwise through the bones into thirds. This will give you strips of 1½-inch ribs.

Combine the remaining ingredients in a large bowl. Add the ribs and rub well with the mixture. Marinate at room temperature for 30 minutes, stirring and rubbing the ribs a few times.

Grill the ribs directly over medium to high heat (350 to 400°F) for 20 to 25 minutes until they become slightly charred. Turn and baste with any remaining marinade several times. Cut into serving portions.

Serves 4

The orange juice mellows the hoisin sauce and adds a slight fruity flavour to the ribs.

I usually serve these as a dinner. But they can also be an appetizer, followed by a light main course, such as a shrimp or chicken salad.

Pork SATAY
with a dipping sauce

Satay is grilled strips of meat on bamboo skewers. This recipe calls for pork, although chicken and beef can be cooked in the same way.

Serve with Satay Dipping Sauce, sliced bananas and cucumbers.

1-lb	piece of lean pork butt roast
2 cups	chopped white onion
⅔ cup	hoisin sauce
½ cup	fresh lime juice
8	large garlic cloves, chopped
2 tbsp	grated fresh ginger
2 tbsp	olive oil
	Satay Dipping Sauce
	bamboo skewers

Soak the bamboo skewers in cold water.

Slice the pork into strips about ¼ inch thick and 6 inches long and place in a bowl.

Combine the onion, hoisin sauce, lime juice, garlic, ginger, and olive oil in a food processor or blender to make a purée of the ingredients. Pour over the meat and marinate for 30 minutes at room temperature. Turn the pieces of meat several times.

Remove the meat from the marinade and pat dry with a paper towel. Thread the meat on skewers and grill directly over medium to high heat (350 to 400°F) for approximately 2 to 4 minutes a side.

Serves 4

Satay dipping sauce

⅔ cup	creamy peanut butter
4 tbsp	olive oil
2 tbsp	fresh grated ginger
2 tbsp	light soy sauce
2 tbsp	lime juice
2 tbsp	honey
2 tsp	dried and crushed red chilies
	hot water

Except for the hot water, put all the ingredients into a food processor or blender. Begin to blend, adding just enough water to make a thin paste-like sauce.

Yields ⅔ cup

Marinated
pork steaks

This recipe requires a 30-minute marinating and about 16 minutes cooking on a hot grill.

4	medium pork steaks (¾ inch thick)
½ cup	olive oil
⅓ cup	soy sauce
⅓ cup	fresh lime juice
2 tbsp	balsamic vinegar
4	large garlic cloves, minced
2 tsp	black pepper
2 tbsp	mustard powder

Trim the steaks of any outer-edge fat and place in a shallow dish.

Combine the olive oil, soy sauce, lime juice, balsamic vinegar, garlic and black pepper. Mix the mustard powder with a little water, making a thin paste. Stir this paste into the other ingredients and mix well.

Pour the marinade over the steaks and allow to stand at room temperature for 30 minutes.

Grill the steaks directly over high heat (400°F) for 8 minutes a side, turning and basting with the marinade. The steaks will be beginning to brown nicely.

Serves 4

Papaya
pork steak

4	medium pork steaks (¾ inch thick)
	liquid honey
1	large papaya
1	large lime
½ tsp	black pepper

Just about any type of fruit goes well with pork. In this one I use papaya only because it is one of my favourite fruits.

Peel, seed and chop the papaya. Put it into a bowl, squeeze the lime juice over it, add the pepper and mash these ingredients with a fork so that they are combined but lumpy.

Trim the fat from the steaks as well as possible, sprinkle with salt and grill directly over high heat (400 to 450°F) for 8 minutes a side, until the outside just begins to char.

Brush liberally with the honey. Spread some of the papaya mixture over top and cook for another 1 or 2 minutes.

Serves 4

Pork tenderloin with
grilled
bell peppers

When on holidays in Santa Rosa, California, I ate a dish similar to this in a Spanish restaurant. Ancho chilies are dried poblanas. They are mild to moderately hot.

I use the indirect method of barbecue cooking with this cut of pork. To avoid overcooking and drying it out, I check the internal temperature with an instant-read thermometer. The barbecuing will take 45 minutes.

2	pork tenderloins (¾ lbs each)
6	large dried ancho chilies
½ cup	olive oil
½ cup	sweet port
2 tbsp	fresh lime juice
1 tbsp	paprika
1 tbsp	white pepper
1 tsp	salt
3 tbsp	plain yogurt
3	large red bell peppers, stemmed and seeded

Remove the stems and seeds from the chilies. Coarsely chop the chilies and soak them in very hot water for 20 minutes until they have softened.

Remove the exterior membrane from the tenderloins.

Combine the chilies, olive oil, port, lime juice, paprika, white pepper and salt in a food processor or blender, and whirl until smooth. If more liquid is needed, add a little of the water that the chilies were soaking in. Pour this marinade over the tenderloins and let stand at room temperature for 30 minutes.

Remove the stems and seeds from the bell peppers, keeping them whole.

Preheat the barbecue to 350 to 400°F, using the indirect method in which only one burner is lit. Have the back burner on with the front ones unlit, or one side burner on with the opposite side unlit.

Place the tenderloins on the unlit area of the barbecue, reserving the marinade in a small saucepan. Barbecue the tenderloins until the internal temperature reaches 145°F and they are lightly charred on all sides, which should take 45 minutes. Turn the tenderloins several times.

At the same time, put the whole peppers on the lit side of the barbecue and cook for 45 minutes, turning often, until they begin to char.

Bring the marinade to a boil. Remove from the heat, add the yogurt and whisk until smooth.

When the tenderloins are done, slice them crosswise every ¾ inch and arrange the slices on a serving platter. Transfer the bell peppers to a cutting board, coarsely chop them and arrange around the tenderloins. Pass the yogurt marinade as a condiment.

Serves 4

Acuna pork steaks

One time I visited Acuna, a small border town in Mexico, where I bought a pork steak from a man who was grilling them by the side of the road. This recipe is as close as I can get to the taste of the one I ate then.

4	medium pork shoulder steaks, trimmed of fat
½ cup	fresh lime juice
2 tbsp	sugar
2 tbsp	cumin powder
1 tsp	salt
½ tsp	cayenne pepper
1	large white onion, cut into ¼-inch rings
	salt

Put the steaks into a resealable plastic bag.

Combine the lime juice, sugar, cumin, salt and cayenne in a jar and shake to dissolve the sugar. Pour the marinade over the steaks, add the onion rings, seal the bag and let sit at room temperature for 45 minutes.

Grill the steaks directly over medium to high heat (350 to 400°F) for about 8 minutes a side, or until the steaks begin to get crispy and charred.

At the same time, put the onion rings on the grill and cook until they begin to char.

Put the steaks on separate dinner plates topped with onion rings. Sprinkle with salt before serving.

Serves 4

Thai PORK
medallions

2	large pork tenderloins (1 lb each)
4	large garlic cloves, sliced
1 tbsp	fresh grated ginger
1	large jalapeño pepper, stem removed
¾ cup	chopped fresh cilantro
¼ cup	port
¼ cup	demerara sugar
2 tbsp	olive oil
1 tbsp	soy sauce
1 tbsp	coriander powder

A variation on a popular Thai dish with ingredients that are easy to find. Just a short marinating and a quick grilling and dinner's ready.

Slice the pork tenderloins crosswise into ½-inch slices. Pound the slices between wax paper to half their thickness and arrange in shallow dish.

Mince the garlic, ginger and jalapeño pepper in a food processor. Add the remaining ingredients and process until creamy. Pour the marinade over the pork and allow to stand at room temperature for 30 minutes, turning the pork several times.

Grill the pork directly over high heat (400 to 450°F) until lightly browned, about 2 minutes a side, turning and basting with the marinade several times.

Serves 4

Pork tenderloin

with Jamaican jerk sauce

This recipe is similar to one that a Jamaican friend prepared for me. She kept most of the recipe a secret, saying it had been in her family for years. I learned what I could from her and guessed the rest.

1	large pork tenderloin (about 1 lb)
¾ cup	dark rum
½	small chopped white onion
6	large chopped garlic cloves
3 tbsp	allspice
2 tbsp	coriander powder
2 tbsp	turmeric powder
1 tbsp	cumin powder
1 tsp	cayenne pepper
1 tsp	salt

Slice the tenderloin crosswise in ¾-inch slices. Put the slices into a dish in a single layer.

Combine the remaining ingredients in a blender or food processor. Process until well blended. Pour over the tenderloin rounds and allow to stand at room temperature for 30 minutes.

Grill the rounds directly over high heat (400 to 450°F) for 3 to 4 minutes a side, turning and basting with the marinade several times.

Serves 2

Pineapple HAM steak

1	centre-cut ham steak (2 lbs, 2 inches thick)
1 cup	sweet sherry
1 cup	canned crushed pineapple
1/4 cup	dry mustard powder
1/4 cup	melted butter
1/4 cup	brown sugar
2 tsp	paprika
1 tsp	clove powder
1 tsp	black pepper
1	garlic clove, minced

This one is for the ham lovers who don't have the time to cook a whole ham. The sweetness of the sherry and pineapple moderate the sharpness of the dry mustard.

To keep the steak from curling, make 1-inch-long fringe cuts around the outer edge, spacing them 1 inch apart.

Combine all the other ingredients and pour this marinade over the ham steak. Allow to stand for 30 minutes at room temperature. Turn the steak several times.

Grill the steak directly over medium to high heat (350 to 400°F) for 25 minutes. Turn and baste frequently with the marinade several times. Carve into individual portions and serve.

Serves 4

Lamb steaks in a

spicy yogurt marinade

Shoulder steaks are probably the least expensive cut of lamb. In this recipe I call for ¾-inch steaks weighing 6 ounces. If you are truly being sold lamb and not mutton, the steaks could not be any bigger than this.

4	lamb shoulder steaks (6 oz each, ¾ inch thick)
2 cups	yogurt
2 tbsp	fresh lime juice
1 tbsp	coriander powder
1 tbsp	cumin powder
1 tbsp	grated fresh ginger
2	large garlic cloves, minced

Place the steaks in a shallow dish in one layer.

Combine the yogurt, lime juice, coriander, cumin, ginger and garlic and mix well. Pour the mixture over the steaks and marinate for 30 minutes at room temperature, turning the steaks a few times.

Grill the steaks directly over medium to high heat (350 to 400° F) for 6 to 8 minutes a side, turning and basting often with the marinade.

Serves 4

LEG OF LAMB
Mexican-style

1	leg of lamb (4 lbs), boned and butterflied
1 cup	olive oil
1 cup	sweet port
¼ cup	fresh lime juice
¼ cup	whole dried Mexican oregano, crushed
8	large garlic cloves, minced
1 tbsp	coarse sea salt
1 tbsp	cayenne pepper

Place the leg of lamb in a non-reactive dish just big enough to hold the meat.

Combine the remaining ingredients and pour over the meat. Allow to sit at room temperature for 30 minutes or cover with food wrap and refrigerate for 3 to 4 hours, turning several times.

Remove the lamb and put the marinade into a small saucepan and set aside.

Put the lamb flat on the barbecue directly over medium heat (350°F) and close the lid. Turn the lamb several times, cooking until both sides are well browned and the internal temperature reaches 160°F. This will give you a medium-to-well-done result and will take 45 minutes to 1 hour. Place the meat on a large serving platter.

Bring the remaining marinade to a boil. Slice the leg crosswise and serve the marinade as a dipping sauce.

Serves 4

Mexicans cook cabrito, the leg of a baby goat, this way. Since goat isn't that easy to find in North America, and you do have to acquire a taste for it, I've substituted lamb.

Ask your butcher to bone and butterfly the leg. You can choose the shorter or longer marinating period; grilling will take 45 minutes to an hour.

LEG OF LAMB
with a BREAD-CRUMB crust

This dish requires grilling and low, slow barbecuing off direct heat. After the meat has been browned, the final cooking will take about 30 minutes.

Most butchers will bone and butterfly the leg for you. By buying lamb legs at 5 pounds or less, you know you aren't getting mutton.

1	leg of lamb (5 lbs), boned and butterflied
10	large garlic cloves, slivered
2 tbsp	coarse sea salt
1/4 cup	fine bread crumbs
1 tbsp	black pepper
1 tbsp	thyme powder
1/4 tbsp	minced fresh mint
	olive oil
1/4 cup	minced onion

Make slits over the entire surface of the meat, rub the surface with sea salt and stuff the slits with garlic slivers.

Combine the bread crumbs, black pepper, thyme and mint. Add just enough olive oil to make a paste, stir the minced onion into the mixture and set aside.

Grill the meat directly over high heat (400 to 450°F) until well seared on all sides, and then remove to a working surface.

If the bread-crumb mixture has thickened, add a little more olive oil. Pat the mixture firmly on the inside (or bone side) of the lamb.

Readjust the barbecue burners for the indirect method of cooking, shutting off 1 and having the other 2 on low to medium.

Put the lamb on the unfired area with the bread-crumb mixture facing up. Cook until the topping is well crusted and the internal temperature is 140 to 150°F. Allow to stand for 10 minutes before slicing.

Serves 4

Lamb kebabs
with red and yellow PEPPERS

4 lbs	lamb, trimmed well
2	large red bell peppers
2	large yellow bell peppers
2	large zucchini
¾ cup	olive oil
8	large garlic cloves, minced
½ cup	fresh lime juice
½ cup	liquid honey
¼ cup	sweet hot sauce (e.g., Tiger Sauce)
3 tbsp	black pepper
1 tsp	dried and crushed red chilies
36	bamboo skewers

These lamb cubes with pepper pieces and zucchini slices, are briefly marinated in a sweet and hot sauce and then grilled. The 10-minute grilling time will produce medium-rare lamb.

Serve the kebabs with potato salad.

Soak the skewers in cold water for 30 minutes.

While the skewers are soaking, cut the lamb into 2-inch cubes. Cut the peppers into 1-inch squares. Slice the zucchini crosswise at 1-inch intervals.

Alternate 3 cubes of meat and pieces of red and yellow peppers and zucchini slices on skewers and place in a shallow dish. You will have about 18 kebabs. To prevent the vegetables from spinning, use 2 skewers parallel and ¼ to ½ inch apart.

Prepare a basting sauce by heating the olive oil, garlic, lime juice, honey, hot sauce, pepper and red chilies in a saucepan over low heat. Stir well and pour over the kebabs. Allow to stand at room temperature for at least 30 minutes.

Grill the kebabs directly over high heat (400 to 450°F) for about 5 minutes a side, turning and basting often with the marinade.

Serves 6

Lemon lamb
KEBABS

Here's another lamb kebab but without the vegetables. These smaller cubes are grilled longer and will be cooked to medium.

2 lbs	lean lamb
¾ cup	olive oil
¼ cup	fresh lemon juice
2 tbsp	balsamic vinegar
2 large	garlic cloves, sliced
1 tsp	coriander powder
¼ tsp	curry powder
	bamboo skewers

Soak the skewers in cold water for 30 minutes.

Cut the lamb into 1-inch cubes and thread the pieces onto 8 skewers. Put them into a shallow non-reactive dish. Combine the olive oil, lemon juice, balsamic vinegar, garlic, coriander and curry in a blender or food processor and whirl until creamy. Pour over the kebabs and allow to stand at room temperature for 30 minutes.

Grill directly over high heat (400 to 450°F) for about 20 minutes for medium.

Serves 4

Poultry

After beef, chicken is probably the most common meat grilled on the barbecue. I prefer to grill the dark meat of chicken. Your timing has to be right on for breasts because they dry out easily. I find grilled breasts lend themselves to treatments where they are sliced or chopped and wrapped in a tortilla or spread on pizza. Another great technique for breasts is my grilled rollups with ham and cheese, which stay juicy.

Chicken legs are more forgiving. You don't have to keep your eye so closely on the timer. I use them in several ways—drumsticks with a spicy dipping sauce, or the thighs basted with honey, soy sauce and garlic. One smart fast method of grilling thighs has them boned and skinned before being marinated. The flavours of the marinade penetrate more of the meat and the thighs grill very quickly.

Not many people think of grilling chicken livers, but I believe that the barbecue is perfect for the quick, hot cooking that livers should have.

Because we're going for fast in this book, there are no recipes for whole chickens. I do give a good Christmas turkey substitute in my Cornish game hen recipe. The birds are halved and then grilled in less than forty-five minutes.

When purchasing poultry, look for skin that is just off-white and has a sheen. The fat should be white. When you press with your finger, the meat should feel plump and firm. It will return to its original shape when released.

Chicken pieces
ON THE GRILL

2	chickens (3 lbs each), cut as above
½ cup	fresh lime juice
¼ cup	olive oil
¼ cup	molasses
1 tbsp	cumin powder
1 tbsp	coriander powder
1 tsp	dried and crushed red chilies
½ tsp	black pepper
½ tsp	salt
¼ cup	minced fresh cilantro

Cut (or have your butcher cut) each chicken into 8 pieces: 2 legs, 2 thighs and 2 breast halves each cut in half. Allow 30 minutes for marinating and 30 minutes, tops, for grilling.

Place the chicken pieces in a shallow dish. Combine the lime juice, olive oil, molasses, cumin, coriander, dried chilies, pepper and salt and mix well. Pour this mixture over the chicken pieces and allow to stand at room temperature for 30 minutes, turning and coating the chicken pieces a few times.

Grill the chicken pieces directly over medium to high heat (350 to 400°F) for 20 to 30 minutes, turning and basting with the marinade several times.

Arrange on a large serving platter and sprinkle with the cilantro.

Serves 4

Chicken breasts
with ginger and hot chilies

With chicken breasts, timing is the key. If they are cooked just a little too long, they can dry out. This marinade helps to keep them moist and gives them a citrus-spice flavour.

8	small chicken breast halves, skinned
1 cup	undiluted frozen orange juice, thawed
2 tbsp	soy sauce
2 tbsp	cider vinegar
3 tbsp	grated fresh ginger
2 tbsp	dried and crushed red chilies

Put the chicken pieces in one layer in a shallow, non-reactive dish.

Combine the orange juice, soy sauce, cider vinegar, ginger and dried chilies and pour over the chicken. Marinate at room temperature for 30 minutes, turning the chicken several times.

Grill the chicken directly over medium heat (350°F) bone-side up for about 16 minutes until the meat just begins to brown. Turn bone-side down and grill for about 4 more minutes, basting now with the marinade.

Serves 4

Salmon Steaks with Lemon and Ginger, p.100

CHICKEN fajitas

8	small chicken breast halves, boned and skinned
3	medium onions, quartered
4 tbsp	Poultry Rub (see page 33)
2 tbsp	minced cilantro
8	flour tortillas (10-inch diameter)

Place the breasts between wax paper and pound them to half their thickness. Sprinkle liberally with the spice rub and allow to stand for 30 minutes at room temperature.

Before cooking, push toothpicks through the quartered onions. Grill them directly over medium to high heat (350 to 400°F), turning often and cooking until they begin to char.

Remove the onions from the barbecue and extract the toothpicks. Put the onions into a resealable plastic bag and seal it.

Grill the chicken breasts directly over medium to high heat for 3 to 5 minutes a side. Remove the chicken to a cutting board, shut off the burners, and put the tortillas into the barbecue to warm up while you cut the chicken into thin slices.

Place the chicken in the centre of a large serving platter and sprinkle with the cilantro. Coarsely chop the onions and arrange around the chicken. Put the tortillas into a basket and pass around.

Serves 4

If I just want the subtle flavour of chicken in a fajita, I spread some sour cream over a heated tortilla and fill it with grilled chicken, grilled onion and a dab of salsa.

In this treatment, I use my Poultry Rub, which doesn't overwhelm the chicken. Pounding the breasts breaks down the fibers so the spices penetrate faster and the grilling is shorter.

Stuffed Sirloin Steak, p. 53

Barbecue chicken PIZZA

As far as I'm concerned, pizza is a snack, but I developed my barbecue pizza for those who consider it a dinner item. This will make one pizza, a dinner for two.

2	small chicken breast halves, boneless and skinless
¾ cup	barbecue sauce, divided
1	12-inch pre-baked pizza shell
¾ cup	shredded mozzarella
½ cup	shredded asiago
1	green bell pepper, thinly sliced
1	white onion, thinly sliced
1 tsp	dried oregano leaves

Grill the chicken breasts over medium to high heat (350 to 400°F) for 15 minutes or until done. Remove to a cutting board and chop into ½-inch pieces and place in a bowl. Add half the barbecue sauce and toss to coat all the pieces well.

Spread the remaining sauce over the pizza shell and sprinkle the mozzarella over top. Arrange the slices of bell pepper and white onion and the chicken pieces on top of the cheese. Sprinkle with the asiago and oregano powder.

Cook the pizza directly over medium to high for about 15 minutes until the cheese has melted.

Serves 2

Chicken rollups with ham and cheese

8	medium skinless, boneless chicken breast halves
	black pepper
	salt
	freshly grated Parmesan
8	thin slices Black Forest ham
8	thin slices prosciutto
8	thin slices provolone
8	pickled asparagus spears
	olive oil
2 cups	yogurt
2 tbsp	coriander powder
1 tbsp	fresh grated ginger
1 tbsp	raspberry vinegar

The procedure here takes a little bit of time but the payoff is a tasty treat.

One at a time place the chicken breasts between wax paper and pound with a mallet until they are about ¼ inch thick.

Sprinkle the breasts with Parmesan, pepper and salt. Place a slice of Black Forest ham, proscuitto and provolone on each piece of chicken. Pat the asparagus spears dry with paper towels, place on one short end and roll tightly. Pin with a toothpick so they don't unroll. Break the protruding ends of the toothpicks off to make the rolls easier to handle on the barbecue.

Combine the yogurt, coriander, ginger and raspberry vinegar. Set aside at room temperature until the chicken is grilled.

Grill the chicken rollups over high heat (400 to 450°F) for about 10 minutes, rolling them gently across the grid and basting with a little olive oil. By the time the chicken is done, it will be starting to brown.

Serve with the yogurt sauce.

Serves 4

Drumsticks with peanut butter dipping sauce

People don't fight over plain grilled drumsticks, but put this dipping sauce on the table and you can expect to see some aggressive eating manoeuvres.

Go easy on the chili peppers, adding them a little at a time, to be sure that the dipping sauce is not too hot

16	medium chicken legs, skin on
4 tbsp	Poultry Rub (see page 33)
1 cup	smooth peanut butter
2 tbsp	fresh lime juice
2 tbsp	oyster sauce
2 tbsp	liquid honey
1 tbsp	olive oil
1 tbsp	dried and crushed red chili peppers
	hot water

Rub the legs with the poultry rub, using it all, and allow to stand at room temperature until you prepare the dipping sauce.

Combine the peanut butter, lime juice, oyster sauce, honey, olive oil and chili peppers in a bowl. Add just enough hot water to produce a consistency that can be used as a dipping sauce.

Grill the legs directly over medium to high heat (350 to 400°F) until they are cooked to the point where the meat is just about falling off the bone. Turn the legs often to get them evenly and well browned. This will take 30 to 40 minutes. Serve with the dipping sauce.

Serves 4

CHICKEN LIVERS
with bell peppers

1 lb	chicken livers, patted dry
1	large green pepper, halved and seeded
1	large red pepper, halved and seeded
1	large white onion, quartered
4 tbsp	olive oil
4	large garlic cloves, minced
2 tbsp	chili powder
2 tbsp	paprika
1 tbsp	black pepper
1 tsp	oregano powder
1 tsp	cumin powder
1 tsp	salt
1/2 tsp	white pepper

Start with fresh, firm livers. Cook them quickly and serve them immediately so they don't lose their crispy texture. That's the secret to grilling chicken livers. To keep the livers from falling into the fire, you may want to use a grill grid.

Combine the garlic, chili powder, paprika, black pepper, oregano, cumin, salt and white pepper in a small shallow bowl.

Dip the chicken livers into the oil and then press them into the spice mixture so that the spices adhere to the livers. Put the livers on wax paper in a single layer.

Push toothpicks through the onion quarters to hold them together. Put them and the bell peppers directly over medium to high heat (350 to 400°F). Grill, turning frequently, until they just begin to char. Remove the vegetables from the barbecue, extract the toothpicks and put the peppers and onions into a resealable plastic bag and seal it.

Raise the barbecue heat to high (400 to 450°F). Grill the livers until well browned, gently turning them several times. This will take 4 to 6 minutes a side. Remove and place in a serving bowl.

Coarsely chop the vegetables and add to the bowl, toss well and serve immediately.

Serves 4

THAI THIGHS

In Thailand you will often see sidewalk vendors serving up deliciously spicy chicken similar to what I've created by replacing some ingredients not easily available in North America. You'll need about 5 to 6 limes for the ⅓ cup of juice.

With the bone removed, the thighs take a very short time to grill.

12	small chicken thighs, boned and skinned
⅓ cup	fresh lime juice
¼ cup	undiluted frozen orange juice, thawed
3 tbsp	port
3 tbsp	hot sauce (e.g., Melinda's XXXtra Hot Sauce)
3 tbsp	fresh grated ginger
2 tbsp	coriander powder
2 tbsp	minced cilantro
1 tbsp	light soy sauce
	salt

Place the chicken in a shallow dish.

Combine the lime juice, orange juice, port, hot sauce, ginger, coriander, cilantro and soy sauce in a bowl, mixing them well. Pour over the chicken thighs and set aside at room temperature for 30 minutes.

Grill the thighs directly over high heat (400 to 450°F) for 10 to 12 minutes, turning and basting with the marinade often. Remove from the grill, sprinkle with salt and serve.

Serves 4

Chicken **thighs**
with honey and garlic

8	medium chicken thighs
2 tbsp	liquid honey
2 tbsp	lime juice
1 tbsp	soy sauce
1 tbsp	coriander powder
1 tsp	hot sauce (e.g., Melinda's XXXtra Hot Sauce)
4	large garlic cloves, minced

I use chicken thighs and legs more often than white meat because the dark meat takes less tending on the barbecue, leaving more room for error.

Rinse the chicken thighs and pat dry with paper towels.

For a basting sauce, combine the remaining ingredients in a bowl, mixing them well.

Grill the thighs over medium heat (350°F), turning the pieces until the skin is crispy and the chicken is done. This will take about 12 minutes a side. Baste with the sauce for the final 5 minutes of cooking.

Serves 4

Spicy chicken wings
with AVOCADO

Even though it's a time-consuming procedure, I remove the skin from the wings. That allows the hot sauce to work directly on the meat.

These are hot, but the avocado mellows them.

20	chicken wings, skin removed
1 cup	hot sauce (e.g., Melinda's XXXtra Hot Sauce)
2 tbsp	fresh lime juice
1 tbsp	cumin powder
1/2	head iceberg lettuce, shredded
2	large avocados, coarsely diced

Combine the hot sauce, lime juice and cumin.

Place the chicken wings in a long-handled, hinged broiler and grill directly over medium to high heat (350 to 400°F) until well browned. Turn and baste with the hot sauce frequently.

Peel and pit the avocado and cut into eighths, lengthwise.

Scatter the shredded lettuce on a large serving platter and surround it with the avocado pieces. Arrange the wings on top of the lettuce and serve.

Serves 4

CORNISH
game hens all spiced up

2	large Cornish game hens, halved
4 tbsp	chili powder
2 tbsp	mustard flour
1 tbsp	dried and crushed red chilies
1 tsp	black pepper
1 tsp	coriander powder
1/2 tsp	salt
	olive oil
4	large garlic cloves, minced

In the firehalls in the Christmas season when we didn't have time to prepare a turkey, we'd grill these game hens, which need 30 minutes to absorb the spice paste and less than 45 minutes to cook.

Combine the chili powder, mustard flour, red chilies, black pepper, coriander and salt, mixing these ingredients well. Stir in just enough olive oil to create a thin paste. Add the garlic and mix well.

Brush the paste on the bone side of the hens and let sit at room temperature for 30 minutes.

Grill the hen halves directly over medium heat (300 to 350°F) skin-side down for approximately 15 minutes, making sure that you do not burn the skin. Turn and grill for another 20 to 25 minutes. The skin should be well browned and crisp and you should be able to wiggle a leg easily.

Serves 4

Seafood

Perhaps the biggest consideration in grilling fish is its texture. Some fish are simply too soft to hold together on the grill. Sometimes, marinating in an acid-based marinade can change the texture of soft fish, making it firmer and easier to handle on the grill.

Generally, however, I prefer to grill firmer-textured fish such as halibut, Arctic char, salmon, swordfish and tuna. We've probably all experienced the strong flavours that seem to hover on the outer edges of pieces of swordfish and tuna. My marinades help to mask those off-moments.

Halibut, being a fairly bland fish, always benefits from the addition of flavour. I offer two recipes based on traditional European methods. One is a moderately spicy Montenegrin marinade; the other is a three-citrus variation of a gremolata, a mix of citrus peel and garlic.

I was a fisherman for many years and I've caught and cooked all kinds of salmon here on the West Coast. Now, with the restrictions on the fishing of coho, I choose sockeye and spring (or chinook) salmon for the recipes I give here. Spring salmon has a little more oil than sockeye, which helps in some of my dishes.

Ask to smell the fish you are buying: bypass anything with a fishy or ammonia odour. The flesh of steaks and fillets should be shiny. As fish is held, even on ice, it tends to lose this appealing shine.

Grilled Arctic **char**

4	Arctic char steaks (1 inch thick)
1/3 cup	olive oil
2	large garlic cloves, minced
1 tbsp	fresh lime juice
1 tbsp	minced fresh parsley
1 tsp	black pepper
1/2 tsp	sea salt

Arctic char range across the northern polar regions. The flavour of this fairly firm white fish is somewhat like its cousin, salmon, and also like trout.

Place the steaks in a dish.

Mix the olive oil, garlic, lime juice, parsley, pepper and salt. Pour this marinade over the steaks and let sit at room temperature for 30 to 45 minutes. Turn the steaks several times.

Grill the steaks directly over medium heat (350 to 400°F) for 4 to 6 minutes a side. Gently turn the steaks several times and baste with the marinade until it is all used.

Serves 4

Halibut steaks
Montenegro style

This is a standard Montenegrin treatment for white fish reflecting the national preference for spicy food. Because some white fishes are not firm enough to cook on the barbecue, I use halibut steak in this recipe.

Although the fish marinates for 45 minutes, the fast cooking time will allow you to have dinner ready in an hour.

4	halibut steaks (1 inch thick)
1/3 cup	olive oil
2 tbsp	brandy
1 tbsp	molasses
1 tbsp	cumin powder
1 tbsp	coriander powder
1/2 tbsp	black pepper
1/4 tsp	celery salt
1/4 tsp	cayenne pepper

Arrange the steaks in a single layer in a non-reactive dish.

Combine the olive oil, brandy, molasses and spices, mixing them well. Pour half this mixture over the steaks. Turn the steaks and pour the remainder over them. Marinate at room temperature for 45 minutes, turning the steaks several times.

Grill the steaks directly over high heat (400°F) until the marinade coating the steaks begins to brown and crust slightly, which should take 6 to 8 minutes a side.

Serves 4

Zesty halibut STEAKS

4	halibut steaks (1 inch thick)
1	navel orange
1	large lime
1	lemon
1/4 cup	undiluted frozen orange juice, thawed
1/4 cup	olive oil
8	large garlic cloves, minced
1 tbsp	coriander
1/2 tsp	black pepper
1/4 tsp	salt

Along the coasts of the Adriatic and the Mediterranean, grilled, baked or poached seafood is often coated with a mix of citrus peel and garlic, which is a gremolata, to add an intense flavour. Here's my three-citrus variation for grilled fish.

Grate the zest from the orange, lime and lemon. Put the three zests into a non-reactive bowl, add the remaining ingredients and mix well. Squeeze the juice from the lime and lemon, and add to the mixture.

Pour the mixture over both sides of the steaks and place in a non-reactive dish. Let sit at room temperature for 30 minutes, turning the steaks several times.

Grill the steaks directly over high heat (400 °F) for 6 to 8 minutes a side, basting with the sauce until it is all used.

Serves 4

Salmon steaks
with LEMON and GINGER

Since we can no longer buy coho, the best salmon for this recipe will be sockeye or spring. I'd choose the latter because it has a little more oil.

4	medium salmon steaks (1 inch thick)
1/2 cup	undiluted frozen lemonade, thawed
2 tbsp	olive oil
1 tbsp	sweet hot sauce (e.g., Tiger Sauce)
1 tsp	grated fresh ginger
1	large lemon

Arrange the steaks in one layer in a shallow dish. Combine the undiluted lemonade, olive oil, sweet hot sauce and ginger. Pour over the salmon and allow to stand at room temperature for 30 minutes.

Grill the steaks directly over medium to high heat (350 to 400°F) for 6 to 8 minutes a side, turning them once gently. Baste with the marinade. Arrange on a serving platter and squeeze the juice of the lemon over top before serving.

Serves 4

Salmon cured and BARBECUED

1	salmon fillet (2 lbs), pin bones removed
1¼ cups	demerara sugar, divided
½ cup	pickling salt
2 cups	water
½ cup	cracked black pepper
2 tbsp	melted butter
2 large	limes

Combine 1 cup of the sugar, the pickling salt and water in a saucepan. Bring to a boil, and then simmer and stir until the sugar is dissolved. Remove from the heat and allow to cool to at least room temperature.

Place the fillet, skin down, in a non-reactive dish just large enough to hold it. Pour the sugar mixture over top, cover with food wrap and refrigerate for 24 hours. If the brine does not cover the fillet, spoon some over top several times.

Remove the fish and rinse well under cold water. Pat dry with paper towels. Combine the black pepper, the ¼ cup of brown sugar, melted butter and the juice of the 2 limes, making a paste. Pat the paste over top of the entire fillet.

Using only 1 or 2 burners, preheat the barbecue to about 250°F.

Place the fillet on the grill over the unfired side. Close the lid and barbecue for about 30 minutes until the sugar is beginning to melt. Turn the flame on directly under the fillet and grill for about another 8 minutes to crisp up the skin and finish cooking the fish.

Slip 2 spatulas between the skin and the flesh and gently remove the fillet to a platter. This makes it easy to serve the boneless, skinless fillet.

Serves 4

The flesh of spring salmon holds together well during barbecuing or curing. This dish will give you the taste of cured salmon combined with a barbecue flavour.

This must marinate overnight.

SALMON FILLETS
in a CAESAR dressing

I was a captain in a firehall where one of the men did a grilled salmon fillet coated in a commercial Caesar salad dressing. At home, I substituted an egg-less version of my raspberry vinegar Caesar dressing and my own lime mayonnaise, for which you could substitute a bought mayo.

1	salmon fillet (2 lbs), pin bones removed
1 cup	Lime Mayonnaise (see page 23)
1/4 cup	olive oil
1 tbsp	raspberry vinegar
1 tbsp	fresh lime juice
2	large garlic cloves, minced
3	anchovies, minced and mashed
1/4 tsp	black pepper
2 tbsp	freshly grated Parmesan

Combine the mayonnaise, the olive oil, vinegar, lime juice, garlic, anchovies, black pepper and Parmesan, mixing them very well.

Spread this mixture on the top of the salmon fillet and grill directly over medium heat (350 to 400°F) for about 25 minutes until the topping begins to brown well. Do not turn the fillet.

Remove the fish from the barbecue by slipping 2 spatulas between the skin and flesh. You will be lifting the fillet off the skin, leaving the skin behind on the grill so that you can serve a skinless fillet.

Serves 4

MARINATED
swordfish steaks

4	swordfish steaks (6 oz each, 1 inch thick)
1 cup	olive oil
1/2 cup	sweet white wine
1/4 cup	balsamic vinegar
1/4 cup	fresh lime juice
4	large garlic cloves, minced
2 tbsp	Worcestershire sauce
1 tsp	Mexican oregano powder
1/2 tsp	bay leaf powder
1/2 tsp	black pepper
1/2 tsp	dried and crushed red chilies

This preparation also works well with halibut, red snapper and tuna. The marinade enhances the flavour of mild-tasting fish and takes the edge off the strong flavour of swordfish, mackerel or tuna. I use a white wine with a sweetness rating of 3.

Combine the olive oil, wine, balsamic vinegar, lime juice, garlic, Worcestershire sauce, oregano, bay leaf powder, black pepper and red chilies in a non-reactive dish. Add the tuna steaks, making sure that they are covered with the marinade. Allow to stand at room temperature for no longer than 30 minutes, turning several times.

Grill the fish directly over medium to high heat (350 to 400°F) for 3 to 4 minutes a side, turning gently and basting often with the marinade.

Bring the remaining marinade to a boil. Place a steak on individual dinner plates and drizzle a teaspoon of hot marinade over each steak before serving.

Serves 4

TROPICAL TUNA steaks

The total cooking time of 4 minutes will leave the tuna steaks rare in the middle. Sometimes parts of a tuna steak can have a strong flavour; the sweetness of the papaya and pineapple help to mask that flavour.

4	tuna steaks (6 oz each, 1 inch thick)
1/2 cup	olive oil
1/3 cup	amber rum
1/4 cup	light soy sauce
1 tbsp	coriander powder
1/2 tsp	black pepper
1	medium papaya
1/2	small pineapple
1	lime, quartered

Combine the olive oil, rum, soy sauce, coriander powder and black pepper and mix until smooth.

Place the steaks in a dish, pour the marinade over top and allow to stand at room temperature for 20 minutes, turning the steaks several times.

Peel the papaya. Cut it in half and remove the seeds. Cut the halves into quarters. Peel the pineapple half and remove the core. Cut the pineapple into spears.

Grill the fruit pieces directly over high heat (400 to 450°F) until they are just lightly browned. Remove and keep warm.

Lower the heat to about 350°F. Place the tuna steaks on the barbecue and grill for 1 to 2 minutes a side.

Top each steak with a quarter of the papaya and a spear of pineapple. Squeeze the juice of a quarter of lime over top.

Serves 4

Crusted MUSSELS
on the grill

32 to 36	mussels
1	large lime
1 cup	fine bread crumbs
4	large garlic cloves, minced
1/4 cup	minced parsley
1/4 tsp	coriander powder
	olive oil

During a holiday in Washington State, I was near a beach where mussels were abundant. I gathered several dozen and steamed them on site. At dinnertime, I completed the cooking on the grill. Since then, I have prepared mussels this way in my backyard.

Scrub the mussels and remove any beards. Put into a large pot with 2 cups of water and steam for about 10 minutes until the mussels have just begun to open up. Make sure they are not completely cooked. Remove from the pot and allow to cool, discarding any that have not opened.

Remove the mussels from their shells and keep a half shell for each one. Place the mussels in a non-reactive bowl. Squeeze the juice of the lime over top and gently toss.

Combine the bread crumbs, garlic, parsley and coriander. Add olive oil a little at a time until the mixture becomes crumbly.

Place a mussel in each of the reserved shells. Pat a 1/4-inch-thick layer of the bread-crumb mixture on top of the mussels.

Drizzle 1/8 teaspoon of olive oil over each mussel. Grill them directly over medium to high heat (350 to 400°F), with the lid closed, for 5 to 8 minutes or until the bread-crumb mixture begins to brown.

Serves 4

Skewered oysters
with yogurt curry DIPPING SAUCE

Because I always prepare ahead, I will have made the dipping sauce the day before I plan to eat these oysters.

To save work, I buy shucked oysters. While the bamboo skewers are soaking, I'll make a salad and then thread the oysters on skewers and grill them.

48	fresh small oysters, shucked
¾ cup	butter
4	large garlic cloves, minced
2 tsp	black pepper
½ tsp	cumin powder
	flour
16	bamboo skewers

Soak the bamboo skewers in cold water.

Pat the oysters dry with paper towels. To prevent the oysters from spinning while they are cooking, use 2 skewers, parallel and about ¼ inch apart. Thread 6 oysters on a skewer and insert the second skewer beside the first.

Prepare a basting sauce by melting the butter in a small saucepan. Remove from the heat and stir in the garlic, black pepper and cumin.

Dust each skewer of oysters in the flour and grill directly over high heat (400° F) for 4 to 8 minutes, or until the frill on the oysters begins to wrinkle. Turn and baste frequently with the sauce.

Arrange on a large serving platter and serve with Yogurt Curry Dipping Sauce.

Serves 4, 2 skewers each

Yogurt curry dipping sauce

1 cup	plain yogurt
2 tbsp	fresh lime juice
1 tsp	curry powder
1/8 tsp	minced habanero pepper
	2 per cent milk
1 tbsp	minced fresh chives
1 tsp	minced fresh cilantro
2 tbsp	salted sunflower seeds
1/2	small lime

Combine the yogurt, lime juice, curry powder and
habanero pepper in a non-reactive bowl. Add just enough
milk to thin the yogurt to a creamy consistency. Stir in the
chives and cilantro. Chill in the refrigerator.

Before serving, bring to room temperature. Stir in the
sunflower seeds and squeeze the half lime over the top.

Serves 4

Prawns
with mustard and curry

Once you have removed the shells from the prawns and put them into the marinade, dinner can be on the table in a little over half an hour. While the prawns marinate, you have time to boil some new potatoes and toss a green salad.

32	large fresh prawns
1/3 cup	grainy Dijon mustard
1 tbsp	cider vinegar
2 tbsp	curry powder
8	bamboo skewers

Combine the mustard, cider vinegar and curry powder in a non-reactive bowl, blending the ingredients well.

Remove the shells from the prawns but leave the tails on. Add the prawns to the mustard-curry mixture, toss and let sit at room temperature for 30 minutes.

Soak the skewers in cold water for 30 minutes or so.

Thread 4 prawns on each of 8 skewers. Grill directly over high heat (400°F) for about 2 minutes a side, turning only once and basting twice with the remaining marinade.

Serves 4

Shrimp
FRIED on the BARBECUE

1 lb	large shrimp, heads left on
1/4 cup	olive oil
4	large garlic cloves, minced
2 tbsp	Old Bay Seasoning
1 tsp	coarse sea salt
1	large lime

Place a griddle top or cast-iron frying pan on the grid of the barbecue over medium to high heat (350 to 400°F). Heat the olive oil on the griddle, add the shrimp, garlic, Old Bay Seasoning and sea salt. Toss the shrimp often, until the shells turn pink and they begin to char. This will take about 2 to 3 minutes.

Squeeze the juice of the lime over top and serve immediately, along with a heavy bread, such as sourdough. To eat: remove the head, suck out the juices, and then pull the tail off and bite into the true flavour of shrimp.

Serves 2

Shrimp are prepared in this way in the coastal regions of southern Europe and some areas of the coast of the Gulf of Texas. If you can't find large shrimp (there should be about 20 to a pound), buy medium-size prawns. Leave the heads on, so that all the juices of the shrimp are retained.

For this recipe I use a cast-iron griddle top, but a cast-iron frying pan works just as well.

CRAB and avocado salad

I buy the crab meat already cooked, but I cook the crab claws and legs. You can steam them for about 8 minutes, or if you prefer, grill them on the barbecue over high heat for the same length of time. After they have cooled, crack the shells so that the meat will be easy to remove at the table.

4	crab claws
4	large crab legs
1¹/₂ cups	cooked crab meat, flaked
2	large avocados
3	large limes
1	head butter lettuce
2 tbsp	minced fresh chives
2 tbsp	minced celery heart centres
1 tbsp	olive oil
8	pickled asparagus spears
4	pickled okra pods
2	large eggs, hard boiled and shelled
2 tsp	grainy Dijon mustard
	salt and pepper

When the crab legs and claws are cool and ready to serve, line 4 salad bowls with the butter lettuce leaves.

Cut the avocados in half, remove the stone and peel off the skin. Spoon out some of the flesh to double the size of the hollow from the stone, and have a snack. Arrange the avocado halves in the centre of the lettuce-lined bowls. Squeeze lime juice over top, using 2 of the limes.

Combine the flaked crab meat, chives, celery heart and olive oil and the juice of the remaining lime and toss gently. Fill the hollowed-out avocados with this mixture, and top each with ¹/₂ teaspoon of grainy mustard.

Garnish each salad with 1 crab claw, 1 crab leg, 2 asparagus spears, 1 okra pod and finally with 2 quarters of an egg. Sprinkle with salt and pepper.

Serves 4

Vegetables

Five of the dozen recipes in this chapter are either grilled or steamed in foil packets on the barbecue. A sixth features brined vegetables cooked in a roasting pan on the barbecue grid. The rest are done in the kitchen as accompaniments to a complete barbecue meal.

The mellow Walla Walla onion is available for only a few weeks here on the West Coast. I've created a tangy basting sauce to be applied to onion halves in the last minutes of grilling.

My Grilled Crispy Potatoes require a grill grid, a perforated Teflon-coated sheet with rims, to keep them from falling into the fire.

Molasses BAKED beans

2 lbs	small white navy beans
1 tbsp	hot sauce (e.g., Melinda's XXXtra Hot Sauce)
1 tbsp	black pepper
½ tbsp	salt
⅔ cup	molasses
½ cup	brown sugar
3 tsp	mustard powder
1	medium smoked ham hock
2	medium onions, peeled and halved

Place the beans in a large shallow pan. (I use a roasting pan because it can go on the stove and into the oven for next day's baking.) Add enough water to cover the beans by 3 to 4 inches and soak overnight.

Rinse the beans and add fresh water to cover them by 1 inch. Bring them to a boil and simmer for 15 minutes. Remove from the heat and gently stir in the salt, black pepper and hot sauce.

Combine the molasses, brown sugar and mustard powder and gently stir into the beans.

Sink the ham hock and onions into the beans, cover with a lid and bake at 300°F for 6 hours.

You may have to add water if your pot is not heavy enough to retain the moisture.

Remove the lid for the final 30 minutes to allow the top of the beans to lightly crust up.

Serves 8

Some people insist on having baked beans with barbecue. This is for them.

After an overnight soaking, the beans can be baked early in the day or a day or 2 ahead of time and kept in the refrigerator where they will acquire even more flavour.

Quick and easy firehall
baked BEANS

Most of us love slow-cooked baked beans but don't have the time to make them. I cook this hurry-up version in the firehall for the same reason. I bet you can fool everyone with it.

3	cans pork and beans (48 oz each), drained
2 lbs	sliced bacon
2	medium onions, chopped
3/4 cup	water
4 cups	chili sauce
2 cups	brown sugar
2 tbsp	black pepper
1 1/2 tbsp	mustard powder

Slice the bacon crosswise every 3/4 of an inch. Fry in a heavy-bottomed stainless steel pot until crispy. Remove the bacon to a bowl and discard all but 1 tablespoon of the bacon fat.

Add the onions and water to the pot, cooking while scraping all the browned bits off the bottom. Add the beans and chili sauce. Cook on a low to medium heat, stirring gently to blend well.

Gently fold in the bacon and the brown sugar, black pepper and mustard powder. Bring to a very low simmer and gently stir several times.

Serves 20

Corn FRITTERS
with nestled niblets

3	large eggs, separated
6 tbsp	milk
$\frac{1}{4}$ tsp	salt
$\frac{1}{4}$ cup	all-purpose flour
$2\frac{1}{2}$ cups	yellow cornmeal
3 tbsp	melted shortening
1 cup	canned corn niblets, drained
	oil for deep frying

Beat the egg yolks in a bowl, add the milk and salt mixing in well.

Whisk in the flour. Stir in the cornmeal until the texture is smooth. Stir in the shortening and corn niblets.

Beat the egg whites until stiff and fold into the cornmeal mixture.

Drop by soup spoonfuls into a deep fryer and cook until golden brown.

Serves 4

The niblets give crunch to these fritters, which are great with any barbecue dinner, or even lightly toasted on the grill the next day for a lunch.

A tall deep fryer with a small circumference reduces the amount of oil needed for deep frying.

Brined
eggplant, peppers and mushrooms

Brining makes the vegetables firmer and easier to handle on the barbecue.

An aluminum foil roasting pan will do for the barbecue cooking, although you may have to shake it more often to make sure the vegetables don't burn.

1	medium eggplant
1	large red bell pepper
1	large yellow pepper
8 to 10	shallots
1/2 lb	shiitake mushrooms
1 cup	sea salt (for brine)
6	large plum tomatoes
10	large garlic cloves
1 tbsp	black pepper
1 tsp	coriander powder
1 tsp	thyme powder
1 1/2 cups	coarsely chopped arugula
2 tbsp	olive oil
1 tsp	balsamic vinegar
1 tsp	fresh lime juice
12	slices sourdough bread (1 inch thick)

Peel the eggplant and cut into 2-inch cubes. Remove the seeds from and coarsely chop the bell peppers. Cut the shallots in half. Quarter the mushrooms and chop their stems. Put these vegetables into a brine (3 cups water to 1 cup sea salt) and refrigerate for 30 minutes. Quarter the tomatoes lengthwise. Peel the garlic and cut in half lengthwise.

Remove the vegetables from the brine, drain well and pat dry with paper towels. Combine the brined vegetables and the tomatoes and garlic in a large, well-oiled barbecue roasting pan. Sprinkle with the black pepper, coriander and thyme. Cook on the barbecue directly over medium heat (350 to 400° F) for 30 to 45 minutes until the vegetables are browned. Gently shake the roasting pan several times.

Brush both sides of the bread slices with olive oil and grill over high heat until lightly browned. Transfer the vegetables to a large serving bowl. Add the arugula, olive oil, vinegar and lime juice. Toss and serve over the grilled bread.

Serves 4 to 6

Open-faced Steak Sandwich with Roasted Garlic, p. 57

Mushroom compote

2 lbs medium mushrooms
1 small red bell pepper
1 small green bell pepper
1/2 large white onion
1/3 cup butter
1 tsp black pepper
1 tsp celery salt

I like to serve this as a barbecue side dish. Compared to other vegetable dishes, it has a long cooking time, which releases all the water from the mushrooms and brings out the full flavour of the bell peppers.

Remove the stems and seeds from the bell peppers and cut them into 1/8-inch thick slices. Chop the onion. Wipe the mushrooms clean with a dry paper towel or a soft brush.

Melt the butter in a large non-stick frying pan. Add the mushrooms and sauté for 15 minutes over medium to high heat.

Add the sliced peppers, chopped onion, black pepper and celery salt and and sauté until the peppers and onion are very limp and begin to caramelize. This will take another 30 minutes.

Serves 4

Tandoori Chicken Strips, p. 3

Glazed
Walla Walla onions

Because Walla Wallas are available for only a short period, this is a summertime dish. The tangy basting sauce balances the mellowness of these onions, which are great with pork.

4	large Walla Walla onions
3 tbsp	HP Sauce
2 tbsp	olive oil
2 tbsp	fresh lime juice
1/2 tsp	black pepper
1/2 tsp	sea salt

To make a basting sauce, combine the HP Sauce, olive oil, lime juice, pepper and sea salt.

Trim the onions and cut them in half crosswise. Put them cut-side up in a single layer in a dish. Drizzle the basting sauce over top and allow to sit at room temperature for 5 minutes.

Grill the onions cut-side down on the barbecue directly over high heat (400 to 450°F) for 5 minutes or until they get slightly charred.

Turn the onions over, lower the heat to medium (350°F) and grill for an additional 10 to 15 minutes. Baste with the sauce until it is all used.

Serves 4

GRILLED crispy
potatoes

8	medium red potatoes
4 tbsp	olive oil
2 tbsp	butter
1/4 cup	minced fresh parsley
2 tbsp	minced green onion
1 tsp	black pepper

Boil the potatoes for 8 minutes, remove from the heat and set aside in the hot water for 10 minutes to finish cooking. Drain the potatoes and allow to cool.

Heat the olive oil in a small saucepan. Stir in the olive oil, butter, parsley, green onion and black pepper and remove from the heat.

Peel and halve the potatoes, and place on a grill grid on the barbecue. Grill directly over medium to high heat (350 to 400°F). Turn and baste with the olive oil mixture frequently until the potatoes are well browned, 10 to 15 minutes.

Serves 4

If you pre-boil the potatoes, they will cook more evenly when barbecued. A grill grid (a perforated, Teflon-coated steel sheet) will keep the potatoes from falling into the fire.

Potato salad
with CORN NIBLETS

This potato salad, with its unusual ingredients, is an adaptation of one served to me in a small Mexican café. It's not necessary to add salt because the pickled jalapeño and okra bring enough salt to the dish. Canned corn contributes more flavour than frozen or fresh-cut niblets.

2 lbs	white nugget potatoes
1 cup	canned corn niblets
4	small plum tomatoes
1/4 cup	chopped cilantro
1/4 cup	coarsely chopped pickled jalapeño peppers
1/4 cup	coarsely chopped pickled okra
1/4 cup	sliced black olives
2 tbsp	olive oil
2 tbsp	fresh lime juice
1 tbsp	sugar
	black pepper

Boil the nugget potatoes in water until tender. This will take 8 to 10 minutes. Drain and allow to cool.

Meanwhile, drain the liquid from the canned corn. Seed, drain and chop the plum tomatoes.

Cut the cooled potatoes into quarters and put into a large salad bowl. Add the corn niblets, tomatoes, cilantro, jalapeño, okra and black olives. Gently toss.

Combine the olive oil, lime juice and sugar in a small jar. Put a lid on the jar and shake to blend all the ingredients and dissolve the sugar. Pour over the salad and toss gently.

Serves 4

POTATO SALAD
with GREEN BEANS and GARLIC

4	medium red potatoes
1 lb	green string beans
2 tbsp	olive oil
1/4 tsp	vinegar
2	large garlic cloves, minced
1/4 tsp	black pepper
1/8 tsp	salt

In most areas of Europe potato salads are made like this. Mayonnaise in potato salads is unheard of, and the salads are served at room temperature rather than chilled.

Cook the whole potatoes in water until tender. Drain and allow to cool.

Tip and top the beans and cut into 1-inch lengths. Simmer, covered with water, for 8 minutes. Drain and place in a salad bowl.

Peel the potatoes, cut into ¾-inch cubes and add to the beans.

Combine the olive oil, vinegar, minced garlic, black pepper and salt in a small bowl and mix well. Pour over the vegetables and gently toss. Cover with food wrap until ready to serve. Gently toss before serving.

Serves 4

SPICY POTATOES
in foil packets

Potatoes, garlic and mustard always make a good combination. I've created a barbecue variation of a potato recipe German immigrants brought to Texas during the 1800s.

12	nugget red potatoes
½ cup	grainy mustard
2	large garlic cloves, minced
1 tbsp	balsamic vinegar
1 tbsp	water
1 tsp	paprika
1 tsp	hot sauce (e.g., Melinda's XXXtra Hot Sauce)
½ tsp	cumin powder
4 tbsp	butter

Whisk the mustard, garlic, vinegar, water, paprika, hot sauce and cumin together in a bowl.

Cut the potatoes into quarters and add to the mustard mixture, tossing well to coat them with the mixture.

Lay out 4 pieces of heavy-duty aluminum foil. Place 1 tablespoon of butter on each. Arrange equal amounts of the potatoes and the mustard mixture on top. Fold the foil around the potatoes and crimp to seal.

Steam the potatoes in the foil packets on the barbecue directly over low to medium heat (250 to 350°F) for 45 minutes to an hour.

Serves 4

Tomatoes stuffed with RICE

4	large firm hot-house tomatoes
1½ cups	cooked basmati rice
3 tbsp	minced parsley
1 tbsp	minced cilantro
2	large garlic cloves, minced
1 tbsp	olive oil
1 tbsp	black pepper
1 tsp	salt

I prefer hot-house tomatoes for this recipe because they are firmer and easier to hollow out and fill. Basmati rice adds its own wonderful flavour.

Cut the top off the tomatoes, making a slice about ½ inch deep. Using a teaspoon and without puncturing the skin, remove and reserve in a bowl as much of the pulp and seeds as you can.

Chop the pulp into small chunks and then drain away any liquid. Add the rice, parsley, cilantro, garlic, oil, pepper and salt and mix well.

Spoon the rice mixture into the tomatoes, filling them well without splitting the skin.

Grill the tomatoes directly over medium heat (350°F) for 10 minutes. Drizzle ⅛ teaspoon of olive oil over each tomato. Raise the heat to high (400°F) and grill directly over the heat until the tomatoes are lightly charred, 7 to 8 minutes.

Serves 4

Grilled STUFFED tomatoes

Plum tomatoes are usually firmer than other types and have less water.

4 large firm plum tomatoes
¼ cup minced shrimp meat
½ cup fine bread crumbs
¼ cup minced parsley
pinch oregano powder
salt
pepper
olive oil

Halve the tomatoes lengthwise and squeeze out the seeds. Place the halves cut-side down on paper towels to remove most of their water.

Combine the shrimp meat, bread crumbs, parsley and oregano in a bowl, mixing them well. Stir in salt and pepper to taste. Blend in just enough olive oil to make the mixture crumbly. Stuff each tomato half with the mixture, pressing it in gently.

Grill the tomatoes over direct medium heat (350 to 400 °F) with the lid closed for 8 minutes. Drizzle about ⅛ teaspoon of olive oil on each tomato, close the lid again and cook for 10 minutes, or until the stuffing begins to crisp up and the tomatoes are slightly charred.

Serves 4

Salads

ARIZONA
avocado SALAD

California and Florida together produce most of the world's avocado crop, but the largest avocado I ever saw, which was about the size of a softball, was grown in Arizona near the Nevada border.

To ripen an avocado more quickly, try putting it into a paper bag with a tomato.

1 or 2 avocados (1 cup diced)
1 cup minced celery heart (ribs and leaves)
¼ cup mayonnaise
¼ cup chili sauce
2 tbsp fresh lime juice
1 tbsp minced fresh chives
       iceberg lettuce, shredded
1 large lime, quartered
½ lb bacon, fried crisp and crumbled

Peel, pit and dice the avocados. Put the avocados, celery heart and chives into a large non-reactive bowl. Mix the mayonnaise, chili sauce and lime juice and combine with the avocados, celery and chives. Toss gently and refrigerate for 20 minutes.

Arrange small piles of shredded lettuce on individual salad plates and spoon equal amounts of the avocado mixture over top. Squeeze the juice of a quarter lime over each and sprinkle with the crisp bacon.

Serves 4

Arugula and CITRUS SALAD

1	large Texas pink grapefruit
1	large blood orange
1	papaya
2 cups	hand-shredded arugula
	black pepper
3 tbsp	fresh lime juice
1 tbsp	olive oil
1 tsp	sugar
1/4 tsp	balsamic vinegar
1/4 cup	pine nuts, lightly toasted

I like the combination of the peppery taste of arugula and the sweetness of the 3 fruits in this salad. Some people find the flavor of this green vegetable too sharp; a good substitute would be fresh young spinach.

Peel the grapefruit and orange and remove the pith. Carefully remove the thin membranes around the grapefruit and orange sections, keeping the sections in one piece. Do this over a small bowl to catch the fruit juices. Put the fruit pieces into a larger bowl.

Peel the papaya and remove the seeds. Slice the fruit into wedges about the same size as the grapefruit and orange sections and add to the bowl. Cover with food wrap and allow to stand at room temperature.

Prepare the dressing by combining the black pepper, lime juice, olive oil, sugar and balsamic vinegar in a jar. Add any fruit juices you have saved. Cover and shake well to dissolve the sugar.

Place equal amounts of arugula on individual salad plates. Arrange the three fruits over top, alternating them in a fan shape. Shake the dressing and drizzle it over the top of the salad and sprinkle with pine nuts.

Serves 4

CAESAR salad
with crisp CROUTONS

I take the classic Caesar to new heights by adding raspberry vinegar and lime juice and by pre-oiling the croutons, which prevents them from becoming soggy. I often use purchased croutons, or I make my own by toasting cubes of white bread in an oven heated to 400 °F.

1	head romaine lettuce
3	large garlic cloves, minced
3 tbsp	olive oil
1 cup	croutons
1/2 cup	olive oil
2 tbsp	raspberry vinegar
2 tbsp	fresh lime juice
2	large egg yolks (see page 158 re raw eggs)
5	large garlic cloves, minced
6	anchovies, minced, then mashed
1/2 tsp	black pepper
1/4 cup	freshly grated Parmesan

Wash, rinse and trim the romaine. Rip into bite-sized pieces, put into a salad bowl and refrigerate.

Combine the minced garlic cloves, the 3 tablespoons olive oil and the croutons in a plastic container, cover with a lid and keep at room temperature. Invert the container several times to coat the croutons with the olive oil mixture.

To prepare the dressing, combine the raspberry vinegar, lime juice, egg yolks, the 5 garlic cloves, the anchovies, pepper and Parmesan in a jar. Cover with a lid and shake to blend the ingredients very well.

Drizzle the dressing over the romaine and sprinkle the croutons over top.

Serves 4

Celery root and carrot
SALAD

3	large carrots
1	small celery root
2 tbsp	fresh lime juice
1½ tbsp	olive oil
1 tsp	sugar

Wash and clean the carrots. Grate them and place in a salad bowl. Wash and peel the celery root. Grate it and add to the bowl.

Add the lime juice, olive oil and sugar and allow to stand at room temperature for 15 minutes before serving. Toss several times during this period.

Serves 4

This light salad goes well with barbecued beef or heavily sauced meats.

Closely related to celery and tasting like it, celery root is also known as celeriac. Only its brownish, softball-sized root is eaten. Look for a root that is firm and without soft spots. Wash it carefully before cooking or grating.

Coleslaw
with ORANGES

This coleslaw is one that my dad made at least once a week. I imagine it came from his Croatian homeland. I've added the orange slices to sweeten it some.

One ingredient not on the list is patience, which you need to slice the cabbage as thin as possible, as if you were taking shavings. Pre-cut coleslaw is simply too chunky.

½ head of green cabbage
2 medium oranges
½ tsp black pepper
¼ tsp salt
2 tbsp olive oil
1 tsp vinegar

Using a sharp knife, cut thin shavings of cabbage and place in a salad bowl.

Peel the orange and remove as much of the pith as you can. Cut the orange in half and slice it very thinly crosswise. Add the slices and any of the juice to the cabbage and toss gently. Sprinkle with pepper and salt. Add the olive oil and vinegar, tossing everything well.

Refrigerate for 30 minutes before serving, tossing several times while it cools and just before serving.

Serves 4

Cucumber SALAD
with CILANTRO and CHILIES

2	English cucumbers
1	small red onion
1	red bell pepper
1	small carrot
1/4 cup	cider vinegar
2 tbsp	sugar
1 tsp	minced fresh cilantro
1/2 tsp	dried and crushed red chilies
1/2 tsp	salt
1/4 tsp	white pepper

What we call an English cucumber is the variety usually grown in our North American greenhouses. It has fewer seeds and is milder than our field-grown cucumbers.

Peel the cucumbers, remove the seeds, cut in half lengthwise and slice very thinly crosswise. Cut the onion in half and then into thin slices. Cut the red pepper in half, remove the seeds, and thinly slice the halves crosswise. Grate the carrot.

Combine the cider vinegar, sugar, cilantro, chilies, salt and pepper in a jar. Cover and shake to dissolve the sugar. Combine the vegetables and the dressing in a large non-reactive serving bowl, toss well and refrigerate for an hour. Toss the salad several times.

Remove from the refrigerator 30 minutes before serving.

Serves 4

Olive
salad IN A TWO-DAY MARINADE

This salad will keep up to 2 weeks in your refrigerator. As the days go by, it will even taste better. Serve it with Portuguese buns and a robust red wine.

3 cups	coarsely chopped pitted green olives
1 cup	sliced pitted black olives
1	small celery heart (ribs and leaves), minced
1 cup	florets of cauliflower
1/2 cup	minced carrots
3/4 cup	chopped mild pickled peppers
1/2 cup	chopped pimientos
1/2 cup	minced fresh parsley
3	large garlic cloves, minced
1 1/4 cups	olive oil
1 cup	fresh lime juice
1 tbsp	black pepper
1/2 tbsp	whole dried Mexican oregano

Lightly steam the celery, cauliflower and carrots for approximately 5 minutes. Remove to large non-reactive bowl to cool. Add the remaining ingredients, gently toss and cover with food wrap. Refrigerate for 2 days, tossing several times a day.

The salad is now ready to eat or you may put the mixture into sterilized glass jars and seal tightly with lids. Store in the refrigerator.

Yields 6 cups

Papaya and **jicama** salad

1	small jicama
2 tbsp	fresh lime juice
2	medium papayas
1/2 cup	chopped green onions
2 tbsp	olive oil
1 tbsp	raspberry vinegar
1 tsp	sugar
1/2 tsp	salt
1	large butter lettuce
	black pepper

Widely used in Mexican salads, jicama is a root vegetable with a white crunchy flesh. Cooked jicama loses its crunch and has a strong nutty flavour. Raw slices should be kept in cold water or sprinkled with lime juice so that they won't turn brown.

Peel the jicama and cut it into 1/2-inch cubes and place in a non-reactive bowl. Add the lime juice and allow to sit for 2 hours, stirring several times.

Combine the olive oil, raspberry vinegar, sugar and salt in a jar. Put a lid on the jar and shake to dissolve the sugar.

When you are ready to serve the salad, peel and seed the papayas and cut them into bite-sized chunks. Put into a large salad bowl along with the green onions.

Pour the dressing over the papaya and toss gently. Add the jicama and lime juice, tossing gently.

Line 4 salad bowls with lettuce leaves and spoon equal amounts of salad over each. Sprinkle with black pepper.

Serves 4

RED onion rings
and KALAMATA OLIVES

The attractively coloured ingredients for this simple European salad are readily found in any season. Some sourdough bread would be handy to sop up the dressing.

1	large red onion
³/4 cup	kalamata olives
1/3 cup	olive oil
2 tbsp	vinegar
2 tbsp	fresh lime juice
1 tsp	balsamic vinegar
1 tsp	black pepper
1/4 tsp	salt
4	large radicchio leaves

Cut the onion into thin slices. Combine the onion slices and olives in a bowl and toss.

For the dressing, combine the olive oil, both vinegars, lime juice, pepper and salt in a non-reactive bowl and whisk well. Pour the dressing over the onions and olives and refrigerate for an hour, tossing several times.

Place a radicchio leaf on each of 4 individual salad plates. Give the onions and olives another toss and distribute equal amounts into each leaf. If there is any dressing left in the bowl, drizzle it over top.

Serves 4

THREE LETTUCES
with WALNUT OIL DRESSING

½	head fancy leaf lettuce
½	head radicchio
1	Belgian endive
3 tbsp	olive oil
2 tbsp	walnut oil
2 tbsp	fresh lime juice
1 tbsp	vinegar
1 tbsp	black pepper
1 tsp	salt
¼ cup	finely chopped walnuts, lightly toasted

There's a double hit of walnut in this easy and quick salad. A walnut oil dressing mellows the slight bitterness of the endive and radicchio, while the toasted walnuts add crunch.

Tear the leaf lettuce and radicchio into bite-sized pieces. Cut the endive lengthwise into thin strips. Toss the salad greens together in a bowl and refrigerate for 30 minutes.

Prepare the dressing by whisking together the lime juice, vinegar, black pepper and salt in a non-reactive bowl. Slowly whisk in the olive and walnut oils.

Sprinkle the salad with the walnuts and drizzle with the dressing.

Serves 4

TOMATO AND cheese salad
with LIME AND MUSTARD dressing

Bocconcini are egg-sized pieces of mozzarella. The cheese will slice more easily if it is cold.

The lime and mustard dressing gives this one a little zing.

3	large vine-ripened tomatoes, sliced
¾ lb	bocconcini cheeses, sliced thin
¼ cup	olive oil
2	large garlic cloves, minced
2 tbsp	balsamic vinegar
2 tbsp	fresh lime juice
1 tsp	mustard powder
½ tsp	black pepper
¼ tsp	salt

Alternate the tomatoes and cheese slices on a serving platter and cover with food wrap.

To prepare the dressing, combine the olive oil, garlic, balsamic vinegar, lime juice, mustard, pepper and salt in a non-reactive bowl. Set aside and allow to stand at room temperature for 30 minutes to meld the flavours.

Drizzle the dressing over the tomatoes and cheese and serve.

Serves 4

Butter lettuce dressing

3 tbsp olive oil
1½ tbsp fresh lime juice
½ tsp sugar

Combine all the ingredients and mix well.

Put lettuce into a salad bowl and refrigerate for half an hour.

Sprinkle the lettuce with salt and pepper and drizzle the dressing over top, toss gently and serve.

Yields enough for 2 servings

The tender leaves of the butter lettuces need a gentle dressing that will not overpower their subtle flavour. I probably use this simple dressing 3 or 4 times a week.

Lime juice and BALSAMIC
VINEGAR VINAIGRETTE

Try this with any green lettuce. The egg yolk will thicken the dressing.

⅓ cup	olive oil
3 tbsp	fresh lime juice
1 tbsp	balsamic vinegar
1 tsp	sugar
1 tsp	black pepper
¼ tsp	salt
1	egg yolk (see page 158)

Combine the olive oil, lime juice, balsamic vinegar, sugar, black pepper and salt in blender and pulse for 30 seconds. Add the egg yolk and blend for an additional 30 seconds. Drizzle over a salad, toss gently to coat all the ingredients and serve.

Yields enough for 4 servings

salsas

ARTICHOKE AND OLIVE
SALTSA

Saltsa is a European term for a relish. Try this over grilled polenta slices, or with a heavy bread, such as sourdough.

1½ cups	bottled artichoke hearts, chopped
1	small white onion, chopped
1	small celery heart (ribs and leaves), minced
¼ cup	olive oil
1 tbsp	capers
1 tsp	dried and crushed red chilies
¼ cup	chopped fresh basil
1 tbsp	sugar
1 tbsp	minced fresh cilantro
1 cup	pitted whole queen green olives
½ cup	chopped pitted black olives
⅛ cup	balsamic vinegar

Heat the olive oil in a large frying pan. Sauté the hearts until they just begin to change colour. Use a slotted spoon to transfer them to a large bowl. Seal with food wrap.

Sauté the onion and chopped celery in the frying pan until limp. Stir in the capers and red chilies and sauté for 2 to 3 minutes more. Combine this with the artichoke hearts and allow to cool.

Add the basil, sugar, cilantro, green and black olives, and the balsamic vinegar and toss gently. Cover with food wrap and refrigerate overnight, tossing the salad several times. Bring to room temperature before serving.

Yields 2 cups

Avocado and pineapple salsa

2	large avocados, in ¼-inch dice
2 cups	fresh pineapple, in ¼-inch dice
¼ cup	minced green onion
¼ cup	chopped fresh cilantro
½ tsp	minced jalapeño pepper
2 tbsp	undiluted frozen orange juice, thawed
2 tbsp	fresh lime juice
1 tbsp	olive oil
¼ tsp	salt

If you enjoy spicier condiments, add more jalapeño pepper. This salsa goes well with grilled chicken and pork.

Put all the ingredients in a bowl, toss well and allow to stand for 15 minutes before serving.

Yields 2½ cups

AVOCADO and
BELL PEPPER
salsa

A fresh Mexican fiesta salsa. Avocados form the base of many salsas and salads in Mexico. This one is ready to eat after a 30-minute melding time. It's good with pork and chicken.

4	large avocados, peeled, in 1/4-inch dice
1/3 cup	fresh lime juice
1/4 cup	chopped red onion
1/4 cup	minced red bell pepper
2	jalapeño peppers, seeded and minced
1 tsp	minced fresh cilantro

Combine all the ingredients in a bowl and toss gently. Allow to sit at room temperature for 30 minutes, tossing several times.

Yields 2 cups

BELL PEPPER SALSA
with green olives

2	large yellow bell peppers, roasted and chopped
1	large red bell pepper, roasted and chopped
3	large plum tomatoes, peeled, seeded and chopped
1/4 cup	chopped pitted green queen olives
2/3 cup	olive oil
2 tbsp	minced fresh cilantro
2 tbsp	fresh lime juice
1	small jalapeño pepper, seeded and minced
1 tbsp	dried and crushed red chilies
1 tbsp	black pepper
1/2 tsp	salt

This will keep up to 2 weeks under refrigeration, or it can be processed in jars, using conventional canning methods.

See page 158 for instructions for roasting bell peppers.

Combine all the ingredients in a bowl, cover and refrigerate overnight. Toss the salsa several times.

The following day, pack the salsa tightly into 1/2 pint canning jars. Ladle equal amounts of any remaining liquid over top, seal and refrigerate.

Allow the salsa to reach room temperature before serving.

Yields 2 1/2 cups

Bell pepper relish in a
paprika sauce

Variations of this condiment are found in Hungary, Ukraine and Croatia, where it is served at room temperature with just about anything that comes off the grill. The blend of olive oil and paprika gives the appearance of a tomato sauce. This will keep for 7 to 8 days.

1	large red bell pepper, seeded and coarsely chopped
1	large yellow bell pepper, seeded and coarsely chopped
1	medium green bell pepper, seeded and coarsely chopped
2	medium onions, coarsely chopped
3 tbsp	olive oil
3	large garlic cloves, minced
1/2 tbsp	dried and crushed red chilies
3 tbsp	paprika
1 tsp	black pepper
1/2 tbsp	salt

Heat the olive oil in a medium, heavy-bottomed stainless steel saucepan. Sauté the bell peppers for about 20 minutes. Add the chopped onion, minced garlic and red chilies. Sauté until the onions are limp.

Stir in the paprika, black pepper and salt, cover with a lid and cook for 5 to 10 minutes, stirring often to make sure nothing sticks to the bottom of the saucepan.

Yields 2 cups

CRANBERRY and ORANGE salsa

3 cups	chopped fresh cranberries
1 cup	chopped oranges
1	small hot red pepper, minced
2 tbsp	liquid honey
2 tbsp	undiluted frozen orange juice, thawed
1 tbsp	chopped fresh cilantro
1 tbsp	fresh grated orange zest

A full fruity flavour to this one. As are barbecue sauces, more and more salsas are omitting tomatoes in favour of a variety of different fruits.

Combine all the ingredients in a bowl, cover and refrigerate overnight. Toss gently several times.

Allow to reach room temperature, tossing before serving.

Yields 4½ cups

Corn kernel relish with RED PEPPERS

I usually prepare this with fresh peaches-and-cream corn kernels that I cut from the cob, but friends have used frozen kernels with acceptable results.

You will need about 5 cobs of corn for the 5 cups of kernels.

5 cups	fresh corn kernels
1	red bell peppers, seeded and diced
1/2	medium onion, minced
2/3 cup	sugar
2/3 cup	water
1/4 cup	vinegar
1/4 cup	apple cider vinegar
1 1/2 tsp	celery salt
1 1/2 tsp	celery seed
2 tsp	flour
1/2 tsp	turmeric

Place the bell pepper, onion, sugar, water, 2 vinegars, celery salt and celery seed in a large, heavy-bottomed pot. Bring to a boil over medium heat and cook for 5 minutes, stirring often.

In a small bowl blend the flour and turmeric with a small amount of water to make a thin paste. Add to the vegetables.

Stir in the corn kernels, bring to a boil and cook for 5 minutes, again stirring often.

Ladle into sterilized jars, seal tightly and refrigerate until ready to use. This relish will keep under refrigeration for 8 to 10 days.

Yields 5 cups

CUCUMBER salsa with RASPBERRY VINEGAR

2	cucumbers, peeled, seeded, in ½-inch dice
½ cup	seeded and ¼-inch diced red bell pepper
½ cup	chopped fresh cilantro
¼ cup	minced red onion
2 tbsp	fresh lime juice
1 tbsp	raspberry vinegar
1 tbsp	olive oil
1 tsp	black pepper
⅛ tsp	salt

Combine all the ingredients in a bowl and stir gently to blend. Refrigerate for 1 hour. Stir gently several times.
   Allow to reach room temperature before serving.

Yields 3 cups

Quick to prepare and refreshing. Because it does not include peppery ingredients, it cools the palate as you eat a hot and spicy main course.

I prefer English cucumbers because they are never bitter.

Nectarine,
papaya and apple salsa

A salsa that goes well with almost anything, but I prefer it with pork or chicken dishes. I always use Granny Smith apples because of their tartness and crunch.

2	large nectarines, peeled, in ¼-inch dice
1	medium papaya, peeled, in ¼-inch dice
1	large apple, peeled, in ¼-inch dice
½ cup	diced white onion
¼ cup	raspberry vinegar
3 tbsp	sugar
1 tbsp	minced cilantro
½ tsp	dried and crushed red chilies

Combine all the ingredients in a large bowl. Cover with food wrap and refrigerate for at least 3 hours. Gently toss during this period.

Yields 4 cups

Desserts

Apple and nectarine
compote

When I prepare this dessert, I use crisp Granny Smith apples. They give a slight tartness to the dish which my family enjoys. Even though they are tart, the port and other ingredients mellow them out.

2   Granny Smith apples
2   firm nectarines
8   large dried apricots, halved
4 cups   sweet port
1/4 cup   demerara brown sugar
1/2 tsp   cinnamon powder

Peel, halve and core the apples. Slice each half lengthwise into 4 wedges. Halve the nectarines, remove the pit and peel. Also slice each half lengthwise into 4 wedges.

Combine the cut fruit pieces, the apricots, port, brown sugar and cinnamon powder in a medium saucepan. Bring to a boil over high heat, lower the heat and simmer until the apples are tender and the apricots have softened. This will take from 8 to 12 minutes.

Put the fruit into a bowl, cover with food wrap and refrigerate until cold. This will take 3 to 4 hours. (You can prepare the day before and refrigerate overnight.)

Spoon the fruit into large wine glasses and serve. You could begin with a dab of ice cream in the bottom of the glass if you wish.

Serves 4

APPLE
and PARMESAN CRUMBLE

½ cup	butter
1 cup	sugar
2	large eggs
1 tsp	vanilla
2 cups	flour
1 tsp	baking powder
1 tsp	baking soda
¼ tsp	salt
1 cup	sour cream
3 cups	chopped apples
¾ cup	toasted and chopped pecans
¾ cup	demerara sugar
2 tsp	cinnamon
3 tbsp	butter
½ cup	freshly grated Parmesan cheese

I love a good apple crumble, but most of them taste the same, and so I changed a few ingredients.

Preheat oven to 350°F.

Combine the butter and sugar, creaming them well. Add the eggs and vanilla and beat until light and fluffy.

Combine the flour, baking powder, baking soda and salt in a bowl. Add the dry ingredients to the creamed mixture, alternating with the sour cream. When well blended, fold in the apples and spread the batter into a greased 13-inch by 9-inch cake pan.

Combine the pecans, brown sugar and cinnamon in a bowl. With your fingers, work in just enough butter to make it crumbly.

Sprinkle this mixture evenly over top of the batter and bake in the oven for 30 minutes. Sprinkle the cheese over top and bake for 5 to 10 minutes more.

Low-cal
banana cream pie

Lots of people don't like tofu, but they probably won't know that's what they are eating in this pie. You don't have to be dieting to jump at this one. I buy prepared graham cracker pie crusts.

2 cups	medium tofu
5	ripe bananas
7 tbsp	fresh lime juice, divided
3 tbsp	liquid honey
1 tsp	vanilla
¼ tsp	cinnamon powder
1	graham pie crust (9-inch diameter)
	nutmeg powder
1 tbsp	fresh grated lime zest

Wrap the tofu in a clean tea towel and place it between two dinner plates. Put a 1-to 2-pound weight on the top plate to press the water out of the tofu. You may have to change towels several times during this operation. Continue until hardly any water is being drained from the tofu. This could take up to an hour.

Before you begin to build the pie, slice 1 of the bananas into ¼-inch rounds. Put the slices into a non-reactive bowl, pour 3 tablespoons of lime juice over them, cover with food wrap and refrigerate for 1 hour. Turn the slices often.

Chop 3 of the bananas into a food processor or blender and purée with the tofu, 1 tablespoon of the lime juice, the honey, vanilla and cinnamon until very smooth.

Without draining the lime juice from the banana slices, arrange them on the piecrust. Spread the tofu mixture over top, cover with food wrap and refrigerate overnight.

Sprinkle the top of the pie with nutmeg. Cut the remaining banana into ¼-inch slices. Dip the slices into the 3 remaining tablespoons of lime juice and arrange on top of the pie. Sprinkle with lime zest and serve.

BELL PEPPERS
with yogurt

2 medium yellow bell peppers
1 cup kiwi yogurt
1 small lemon
sugar

After tasting the sweetness in raw yellow bell peppers, I decided to dress them up and bring them on as a dessert. This is light and pretty.

Leaving the stem on, slice the peppers in half lengthwise. Clean out the seeds and remove as much of the white membrane as possible and set aside.

Stir the juice of the lemon into the yogurt and hold in the refrigerator.

Grill the bell pepper halves directly over medium to high heat (350 to 400° F). Turn and grill until they just begin to get supple and char slightly.

Remove to individual small dessert bowls. Sprinkle sugar inside each pepper, and fill with the yogurt-lemon mixture.

Serves 4

SIMPLE
blueberry cake

This one is easy, and always a treat when blueberries are fresh.

1/2 cup	butter
1 cup	sugar
3	large eggs
3/4 cup	milk
2 cups	all-purpose flour
2 tsp	baking soda
1 tsp	fresh lime juice
1 cup	fresh blueberries
1/4 cup	brown sugar
1/2 tsp	cinnamon

Preheat oven to 350°F.

Grease an 8-inch by 8-inch cake pan.

Cream the butter and sugar in a bowl. Add the eggs 1 at a time, beating well after each addition. Add the milk, flour and baking soda, beating into a batter.

Stir in the lime juice. Gently fold the blueberries into the batter and spread into the pan.

Combine the brown sugar and cinnamon and sprinkle over top of the batter. Bake in the oven for 30 to 35 minutes. Cool on a cake rack.

Grilled PINEAPPLE rings

1	medium pineapple, peeled and cored
½ cup	undiluted frozen orange juice, thawed
⅓ cup	fresh figs, minced
2 tbsp	dark rum
	black pepper
1	small lime

The grilled pineapple is enhanced by the flavour of the figs and orange juice. Try a European deli for fresh figs; they are available just about year-round.

Slice 4 one-inch-wide rings of pineapple and set aside.

In a small saucepan, simmer the orange juice, rum and figs over low heat for 2 to 3 minutes. Keep warm on low heat.

Grill the pineapple rings directly over medium to high heat (350 to 400 °F) for about 3 minutes a side until grill marks appear on the fruit.

Put the slices on dessert plates and sprinkle with black pepper. Spoon equal amounts of the fig sauce into the centres of each pineapple. Squirt lime juice over top.

Serves 4

SWEET papaya
topping

I love papayas. In Arizona, Texas and Mexico I've bought papayas that weighed more than 5 pounds. I'd eat a half for lunch with just a little bit of salt, pepper and a squeeze of lime juice.

With this recipe I can have papaya ready to eat as a topping on ice cream or a light cake.

1 or 2   papayas (3 lbs in all)
2 cups   water
2 cups   brown sugar
1   lime

Cut the papayas in half, remove the seeds and peel with a sharp knife. Cut into 1½-pieces, place in a bowl and set aside.

Combine the water and sugar in a medium saucepan, bring to a fast simmer and cook until the sugar is dissolved. This will take about 5 minutes and a little stirring.

Remove the sugar mixture from the heat and squeeze in the juice of the lime. Pour over the papaya pieces and set aside to cool. The topping is now ready to use.

If the fruit is covered with the liquid and covered with food wrap, it can be held for 3 to 4 days under refrigeration.

Serves 4

Papaya ICE

1 or 2	papayas (3 lbs in all)
2 tbsp	fresh lime juice
¼ cup	icing sugar
½ tsp	vanilla extract
5 cups	crushed ice

Halve the papayas, clean out the seeds and remove the peel. Chop the fruit. Put the papaya and the other ingredients in a blender. Blend to a slush and serve in large goblets with fat straws.

Serves 4

This is one of my favourite summer refreshers. If you prefer adding alcohol, rum goes very well with papaya. Add 1/2 cup of amber rum, omit the vanilla, and reduce the ice to 3 cups.

IN MY
Pantry

Here are some standard preparations for ingredients often called for in my recipes and a list of the brands of staple ingredients I have in my cupboards.

Roasted garlic

Slice off just enough of the top of a large garlic head to expose the cloves. Put the head on a piece of aluminum foil. Sprinkle the exposed cloves with some paprika and drizzle with a quarter teaspoon of olive oil. Wrap tightly in foil and bake for 25 to 30 minutes at 350°F. Cut the foil open to expose the garlic and allow to cool. Squeeze the cloves to remove the soft garlic.

Roasted red bell peppers

Cut the stems off and using a teaspoon scrape out the seeds. Grill the peppers on the barbecue over high heat (400°F) or broil in the oven until the skin is charred all over. Place in a sealable plastic bag for 10 minutes. Remove from the bag and allow to cool. Peel off the charred skin. To store: cut into smaller pieces, put into a jar, cover with olive oil and keep in the refrigerator for 3 to 5 weeks.

Raw eggs

If you are reluctant to eat uncooked eggs but want to make dressings that call for them, you must first pasteurize the eggs. Eggs cook at 180°F. The *salmonella* bacteria die instantly at 160°F, or can be killed by heating the eggs for 3 1/2 minutes at 140°F. I carefully lower a *room-temperature* egg into boiling water, lower the heat and hold at simmer just until the whites are cooked (4 minutes); the yolks will not be cooked but will have been heated hot enough to kill the bacteria.

Another method that also works: heat 2 yolks, 1/4 cup of liquid from the recipe, and 1/2 teaspoon sugar over very low heat in a small skillet, stirring constantly. At the first sign of thickening, remove the pan from the heat, keep stirring, and immediately dip the pan bottom into a larger pan of cold water to stop the cooking.

Tellicherry pepper

Tellicherry is a port on the Arabian Sea coast of India which has given its name is to a grade of pepper. Tellicherry is a high-quality grade of large peppercorns with a bold, complex taste. I use it all the time, but specify it for only a few recipes, for which I think it is essential.

Salt

I use sea salt all the time and prefer the Baleine brand, particularly their coarse crystals. In the recipes, I call for sea salt only when it's essential.

Balsamic vinegar

Balsamic vinegars, imported now from several countries, can range from $5 to $100 a bottle. Longer aging reduces the acidity, increases the sweetness and thickens the consistency. I buy 2-year-old and 7-year-old Duke of Modena, using the older vinegar for special dishes. I also have a teaspoon of it every morning.

Dried tomatoes	Sonoma, packed in olive oil
Horseradish	Beaver Hot and Beaver Regular
Hot pepper sauces	Melinda's XXXtra Hot Sauce
	Perri Perri Sauce
	Tiger Sauce
	Tabasco Habanero Sauce
	Tabasco Original Hot Sauce
Prepared mustard	Beaver Old English Hot
	French's Regular
	Grey Poupon
	Maille Old Style (grainy)
Olive oil	Bertolli
Sea salt	Baleine coarse crystals
Seafood seasoning	Old Bay Seasoning
Worcestershire sauce	Lee & Perrins

Index